THE HISTORY OF

CULTS

FROM SATANIC SECTS TO THE MANSON FAMILY

THIS IS A CARLTON BOOK

This edition published in 2019 by Carlton Books
An imprint of the Carlton Publishing Group
20 Mortimer Street
London W1T 3JW

Design © Carlton Books 2019

A CIP catalogue for this book is available from the British Library.

ISBN 978-1-78739-268-7

Printed in Dubai

10 9 8 7 6 5 4 3 2 1

Cover photographs: Alamy, Getty Images, Carole Raddato, Rex Features
& Shutterstock

THE HISTORY OF

CULTS

FROM SATANIC SECTS TO
THE MANSON FAMILY

ROBERT SCHROËDER

CARLTON
BOOKS

CONTENTS

INTRODUCTION

Hardly a week goes by without a report in the press covering an incident that is traceable to the activities of a cult. Yet the background to these headline-catching incidents is only rarely penetrated and the organizations responsible go on their way unscathed and largely unseen, continuing to attract devotees. The destruction that can be wrought on individuals and their families and friends is often far-reaching.

Prior to the millennium there was an explosion of interest in cults, particularly among younger, more impressionable members of society; few regions of the world have escaped notice. The phenomenon of the cult has always been with us, though for differing reasons. An explanation of why fringe religious groups are nothing new is perhaps to be found in the editorial column of the *Daily Mail* for 24 February 1996, dealing not with sectarianism but with the right of Moslems to segregate religious education. The article concludes that, "The tenets of Christianity – indeed of Islam and Judaism too – have never been more urgently needed. Honesty. Fidelity. The integrity of the family. Charity toward the less fortunate. These are the values which underpin all civilized societies. And these are the values so conspicuously lacking in the rootless, shiftless, feckless and often amoral youngsters emerging in such numbers from our educational system. The tragedy is that generations of British children in state schools are being fobbed off with ersatz religion, stripped of faith, meaning or commitment."

It is not just in Britain that such criticism applies. It is equally valid whether one examines current values in the USA, Russia or Japan. Nor is this criticism particularly new, although the media may make it appear so. The collapse of religious values has regularly plagued civilization. Little wonder, therefore, that many in today's societies, finding themselves spiritually and morally lost, seek alternative routes to faith and the meaning of existence. Cults have also become more politicized then ever before. Most noticeably in the USA and Japan, the so-called lunatic-cult fringe is convinced, collectively, that it needs to change the world's political order, to achieve dominance and save at least some of humanity's suffering.

A brief but telling insight into the power of cultic belief is to be gained from another, even older, newspaper report. On 2 November 1984, with the Cold War still in full spate, the *American National Catholic Reporter* made reference to ex-President Reagan's espousal of so-called "nuclear dispensationalism". This is the view – held by many Evangelical Catholics – that in the seconds before Armageddon, the righteous will be lifted into the air to greet the Lord and thus be saved from the holocaust. Atomic fatalism characterized much of Catholic right-wing thinking during the 1970s and 1980s, giving rise to the philosophy that avoidance of nuclear war through détente was not possible – the only salvation lay in the hands of the Virgin Mary. That this philosophy may also have been subscribed to by a US president offers a sobering scenario.

Most of the cults that exist today cannot claim to be original, however off-beat they appear to be. Many imitate, in one way or another, older models. Thus the modern Adventists who confidently predicted the end of the world on such and such a date were merely reiterating a time-honoured cliché going back, at least, to the Biblical books of Daniel and Revelation. These two sources alone have been regularly analysed through the ages and have provided fuel for an ongoing assortment of interpretations as to how, when and why the world will grind to a cataclysmic halt.

Most cults offer an escape route to salvation, a special "nod from God" handed out to their devotees, which orthodox faiths, so it is claimed, fail to supply. They are the sane ones; the rest of us are the lunatics bound for annihilation. It is in this belief, this sense of moral and spiritual superiority, that much of their strength lies. Yet it is also the source of their weakness and, if history is any judge, of their ultimate demise.

The purpose of this book is to offer an insight into the workings and mentality of cults and sects, past and present, to examine some of the personalities who invent and build off-beat religious movements and to chart the fate of the disciples who staff them.

ROBERT SCHROËDER

ANCIENTS

Religion was part of the nuts and bolts of earthly existence to the peoples of the ancient world. So how does religion relate to, and differ from, the cult, which the popular mind often associates more with the ancient than with the modern? The *Chambers English Dictionary* provides at least two definitions of the word cult. Primarily it is a system of religious belief, a formal style of worship. Only secondarily is it a sect or an unorthodox or false religion characterized by an often excessive admiration for a person or idea. To the peoples of past eras, the first definition would be more accurate, not least because they had little concept of beliefs that could be considered unorthodox or false. It was only with the rise of the monotheistic religions – Judaism, Christianity and Islam – that the proprietary claims began to emerge.

These were epitomized by the Judaic edict, the second of the Ten Commandments, that, "Thou shalt have no other gods before me" (Exodus 20:2). The cults investigated in this section were, in their day, part of the fabric of society. A cult provided the mainstream form of worship for a community or could meet the spiritual needs of a minority group. The cults of the ancients can be measured in their tens of thousands, but most passed into obscurity without leaving any mark upon history, and the record of only a handful has survived. These are just some of them.

ANCIENT CULTS AND SECRET CAVERNS

The cults of ancient peoples often reflect beliefs that go hand in hand with a reverence for, and a fear of, the awesome might of nature. However, the gulf between our way of thinking and theirs is an enormous one and it can make their articles of faith difficult to understand.

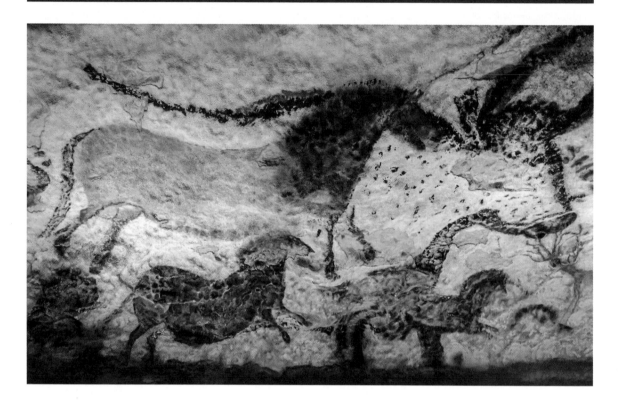

Their uncompromising world of elements, rocks, sky, plants and animals was seen to be part of a common frame that was strong, self-sufficient and at one with itself; a world in which the members of these cults were often the vulnerable and timorous participants. The ancients saw spiritual strength in the immovability of a mountain, a brilliant shaft of light, a great storm, or the indomitable resilience of a bear, a lion, a bull, or a stag. These things were the physical extremities of a greater unseen potency, of which the human intruder was not a part, but instead a captive who was bound by the limitations of his own physical and mental frailty.

THE FIRST CULTS

The people who inhabited the misty edge of prehistory were adventurers – pioneers possessed by a driving energy and curiosity, exploring and fighting to master a new and unfamiliar world. They saw that tremendous forces existed in nature and they believed that if they reached out far enough and strongly enough for answers to their curiosity and needs, the spirits residing in and directing those forces might, just might, be prepared to meet them halfway. The pathway to that meeting point was through their myths and rituals, which involved relating and acting out the deeds of the spirit world and the propitiation of its unseen members. It was a dangerous road but one that, if correctly and successfully followed, could bring great power to its band of journeymen thus, the first cults were forged.

Today's scattered remnants of hunter-gatherers see their world as having both earthly and spirit form. It is as if the mind has recognized the twofold nature of its own being and applied the same principle to all of nature. The hunter recognizes the spiritual power of animals and knows that hunting and killing may bring down the wrath of the creature's spirit guardian, so animals are not sacrificed as an excuse for blood-letting but in a sincere desire to appease the spirits.

Once the need for hunting had passed – with the rise of agricultural civilizations – and humankind's interest became more closely focused on the possibility of life beyond the grave, it is not impossible to see how the animal sacrifice came to be substituted by a human one. There also grew an increasing interest in the plant kingdom, since the green world was seen to be fertilized by the rain from the skies – the semen of the gods – and was therefore possessed of its own particular spirituality.

THE RISE OF THE CULTIC PRIESTS

It needed a certain kind of intellect and intelligence to enter the dangerous realm of intercession with the spirit world and those who did so, in accepting the challenge, took on a certain elitism. They became distinct from the uninitiated and with their elitism came power. The tribal shaman came into being, from whose simple origins and devices – telling the great myths of godly heroes and dressing in animal skins to emulate the beasts of the chase – was to emerge the cultic priest. In order to preserve their powers, these go-betweens developed an aura of mystery and distance and with it came an understanding among lesser mortals that their fate in life, and beyond, rested in the hands of the chosen few. If they had done wrong in the eyes of the gods they would be punished; if they fell sick it was evidence of divine disfavour; if their blood was to be spilled to appease some terrible and hungry luminary, then so be it. Their gods, despite being largely unseen, possessed human attributes. They ate, drank, slept, were happy or angry, fought, fell in and out of love, had sex, went to the lavatory and even died, though rarely for very long. Thus their "human" needs were met with a constant supply of flesh, blood, weapons, sacrificial virgins and other forms of appeasement through the hands of the cultic priests.

Among the very first of these visionaries were the extraordinary architects of the painted sanctuaries who created their masterpieces amid the rigours of the European Ice Age. Deep in the earth of southwest France, where primeval waters carved out vast subterranean halls, are the world's earliest-known art galleries, in which the hunters left an awesome legacy of their reverence for the natural world. In places marked by great isolation from the outside world, and in Stygian darkness broken only by flimsy tallow lamps, the first cultic priests painted animals by the tens and hundreds; they created anthropomorphic figures on the limestone walls beside impressions of human hands, genitalia and other designs too occult to determine. These places, far from normal habitation and often accessible only after negotiation of miles of tortuous passageways, underground rivers, cliffs and crevices, were perhaps the first cult temples where the spirits of the chase were invoked and pleas for survival were uttered deep beneath the world of endless snow and ice.

"Step into one of these antediluvian halls and answers touch you with an almost heart-stopping blow. There is an immensity of nature. Time and inexorable force have sculpted the elemental earth into a myriad of features that are beyond the wit of man. Phantasmal beasts loom from every angle and monstrous organ pipes soar into infinite space. They defy the norms of architecture, and beneath them the human spirit is dwarfed and yet uplifted. They are places of the gods."

Gods of the Earth,
Michael Jordan

Opposite: Wall paintings from the Lascaux Cave, Vezere Valley, France. Dating from c.15,000 BC.

THE CULT OF THE SACRED TREE

The Assyrians of the ancient civilization of Mesopotamia can claim to have brought the strange cult of tree worship to its most glittering climax in the ninth century BC, during the reign of Assur-nasir-apli II.

He ascended the throne of the Assyrian empire in 884 BC and was responsible not only for terrorizing most of the known world with his excesses, but also for rebuilding the fabulous city of Kalakh, the Calah of Genesis, which lies on the northernmost tributary of the Tigris, near the modern Iraqi city of Mosul.

This form of tree worship had probably begun with the carrying of a small plant or tree branch to represent the presence of the fertility or vegetation goddess but, as time went by, it progressed into a full-blown rite involving a highly stylized and decorated totem known as the asherah. This is the object, vehemently criticized among the biblical prophets in Israel, that came to be described euphemistically by the English translators of the Old Testament as "the grove". The asherah, the image of the pagan goddess whose worship so many of the Israelite kings such as Ahaz and Menasseh found seductive, was an "'unspeakable abomination" in the eyes of the religious leaders but its cult carried, nevertheless, a huge following. There is evidence of its popularity in the Old Testament's First Book of Kings. The prophet Elijah challenged the idolatrous King Ahab to match 450 prophets of Baal and 400 priests of the asherah against the Israelite god, Yhwh. While the prophets of Baal met an untimely end, drowned in the River Kishon, the priests of the asherah apparently went unharmed.

HONOURING THE SACRED TREE

Back in the Assyrian city of Kalakh the evidence for the impact of the tree cult is remarkable. The ruins, which were excavated in the late nineteenth century, were found to include a superb palace covering 10,000 square metres (107,640 square feet). The walls of the staterooms in this northwest palace were decorated with plaques, the theme of which was the oddly stylized sacred tree,

before which the king and his courtiers were seen kneeling or standing in homage. Behind the throne hung a magnificent relief, above which hovers the famous winged disc that the Assyrians had borrowed from Egyptian tradition. The sacred tree holds centre stage while the king and a winged god face it in a mirror image of worship.

That the absolute ruler of this immensely powerful kingdom went on his knees before such a quaint bushy object is made all the more remarkable when set against his reputation as a ferocious man of steel. Yet autocrats who succeeded him, and who were so absolute in their power that they ascribed to themselves the title "Great King of the World", also went on their knee in homage. Facsimiles of the rituals by which the tree was honoured were carried in the pockets of princes, merchants and scribes. Paradoxically, though, we are left with not a single line of clear explanation of the tree cult. It is possible that it originated with an ancient Sumerian tradition that tells of Inanna, the Queen of Heaven, taking a tree that grew on the banks of the River Euphrates as her symbol; however, this can never be more than an educated guess. It would seem that the Mesopotamians covered their tracks well.

Ironically, much of the light shed on tree cults comes from the Bible. It is known from the Old Testament that the tree was made from wood and metal adorned with precious stones and bunting and that it bore little relation to a living object. A revealing description from Jeremiah notes that:

[T]he customs of the people are vain: for one cutteth a tree out of the forest, the work of the hands of the workman with the axe. They deck it with silver and with gold; they fasten it with nails and with hammers, that it move not. They are upright as the palm tree, but speak not; they must needs be borne because they cannot go.

Above: The ancient Assyrian capital Nineveh, by Layard.

SACRED SYMBOL OF FERTILITY

There are strong hints that the tree represented the goddess of life, the Queen of Heaven, because its design seems to have incorporated fertility symbolism. The leaf-like palmettes, with which it is decorated on the plaques from Kalakh, reflect the ancient notion of a womb divided into seven compartments, and in the depictions, the king is often seen to approach the tree with a bucket and a phallus-shaped cone. It may be that he represents the sacred guardian, the Gardener, who alone is permitted to enter the shadow of the goddess as her high priest and perform a ritual of fertilization using sacred water – the semen of the gods – and a symbolic phallus with which to apply it.

The legacy was passed on to the Babylonians. It seems that the image of the tree was carried in sacred procession during the Akitu festival, the great Babylonian rite of spring that included the dramatic reconstruction of the creation epic and the symbolic death and resurrection of the king. The festival would reach its climax with the Sacred Marriage – the public intercourse that took place between the king and the earthly representative of the goddess, the lukur priestess.

To what extent these antique cults influenced the Christian idea of the Tree of Life is uncertain, although it is well recorded that tree worshipping rituals were being practised in the Holy Land two centuries after the beginning of the Christian era.

OSIRIS AND THE CULT OF THE DEAD

According to the mythical traditions of Ancient Egypt, the corn god, Osiris – who was both consort and brother to Isis – became the subject of a murderous assassination plot by his jealous brother, Set. Having failed to dispose of Osiris by incarcerating him alive in a coffin and sending him off to a watery grave in the Nile, Set found Osiris's corpse and hacked the body into 14 pieces.

Prior to his dismemberment, however, and through the magical arts of Isis, Osiris became the posthumous father of the Sun god Horus, who subsequently avenged his father's death in a ferocious battle with Set. When Horus had won the day, the divine judges proclaimed him to be – in life – king of the two kingdoms of Egypt. His father, Osiris, took the new role of ruler and judge of dead souls in the Underworld, through which every Egyptian aspired to pass en route to the paradise land of Duat when his mortal span was at an end.

Thus arose the curious Cult of the Dead, practised at many places in Egypt but perhaps mainly at Abydos and Denderah, towns on the Upper Nile some 65–80 kilometres (40–50 miles) north of the city of Thebes, and at Busiris in the Nile delta. It is known that, at Abydos, there stood an elaborate cult shrine built from cedarwood and inlaid with gold, bronze and lapis lazuli in which reposed a gold encrusted statue of Osiris. The cult probably became popular from the Middle Kingdom period in about 1900 BC. Its devotees believed that, at the point of death, their characters would be judged by Osiris and his assessor gods to determine whether their souls would be lost forever or pass on to Duat.

"these rags on my face. Open my mouth. Unbind my legs. Give me charms and incense and cake. Pry open my mouth … I will speak of days unending heaven."

The Egyptian Book of the Dead
Normandi Ellis

Right: Pharaoh of the Eighteenth dynasty, Amenhotep IV, also known as Akhenaton, worshipping sun god Aten.

CULTIC RITUAL

The texts that account the details of the cult festival are perhaps deliberately obscure, but seem to have taken place annually for 18 days between the twelfth and thirtieth of the month of Khoiak. In one of its more public and formal aspects, a ceremonial boat was taken down the river in procession, carrying the god and his shrine, headed by the jackal god Wepwawet. On this journey, the barge was symbolically attacked by priests, who represented the god's adversaries, until it reached the sacred shore at the spot where Osiris himself was reputed to have been slain and where his adversaries were slaughtered. The god was then returned in triumph to his temple. Other texts suggest that the festival opened with a ceremony of ploughing and sowing when two black cattle were yoked to a plough made of tamarisk wood and blackened copper, while a child scattered corn seed. The rituals also involved burying an effigy of Osiris – made from cloth stuffed with corn – in a mulberry-wood coffin after first exhuming his effigy of the previous year, which by this time had sprouted shoots, symbolizing the god's resurrection.

There were lighter sides to the cult's activities. In death one important area of his anatomy remained fully functional. Thus, women paraded through the streets singing and imaginatively operating puppets of Osiris.

THE CULT OF AKHENATEN

One could be forgiven for believing that monotheism – the worship of one god – had been exclusive first to Judaism, before passing to Christianity and Islam. However, monotheism probably owes its origins to ancient Egypt. From 1379 BC to 1362 BC, during the time that the Israelites lived there, the country was ruled by Amenhotep IV. He substituted a universal and virtually exclusive supreme god, Aten, for the traditional polytheistic pantheon headed by the creator god Amun at Thebes, and the Sun god Re at Heliopolis. So convinced was Amenhotep of the existence of this supreme deity that he changed his name to Akhenaten, meaning literally, "raising the high name of Aten".

No icon of this super-deity was allowed but, in Akhenaten's imagination, the god was symbolized by the disc of the sun, first winged and with outstretched hands in imagery made famous by various Hollywood movies, and then more stylized with the cobra symbol of the goddess Wadjet – the preserver of royal authority in Northern Egypt – on its lower rim, and with thin human arms extending toward the Earth as rays.

The origins of this obscure cult lie earlier in Egyptian history. The word aten means "the disc of the Sun", but the god Aten and the notion of the pharaoh returning to his creator, the Sun, was in use in at least 2000 BC. Amenhotep III initiated the cult of Aten at Heliopolis, but it is arguable that under Akhenaten, one of whose queens, Nefertiti, was also a staunch worshipper, the interest was as much political as one reflecting religious fervour. During the reign of one of Amenhotep III's predecessors, Tuthmosis IV, the priesthood of Amun had been allowed to usurp its powers and had begun a conflict with the pharonic royalty that was destined to become increasingly embittered. Eventually, these priests achieved such huge influence that they began to curb the authority of the pharaohs, at which point Akhenaten dismissed them. He built a cult sanctuary adjacent to that of Amun, in the Karnak complex at Thebes, and then a vast centre at el-Amarna, where the temple was open to the sky – the main rituals taking place at dawn. The cult survived for a few decades only, after which Akhenaten's successor decreed that all reference to it should be dismantled. It represents, nevertheless, a radical religion that triggered great cultural disturbance and innovation in Egypt. Whether it is to be seen as the result of one man's political motivation or the culmination of the first religious quest for a single omnipotent god is debatable.

CULTS OF
JUDAISM

Throughout the turbulent history of the Jews, a number of breakaway sects have arisen and vanished, beginning from the moment when Aaron elected, unadvisedly, to introduce a bull cult to the Israelites in Moses's absence. However, no Judaic cult has perhaps been more significant than that of the Essenes, which arose at almost the close of Israelite history.

This cult, interest in which resurfaced in modern times as a consequence of the discovery of the Dead Sea Scrolls, comprised a community of extreme, radical ascetics who became established in a remote area on the Dead Sea coast in around 200 BC and could have continued to practice until as late as AD 200. According to the writer Joseph Campbell, they may have been a fundamentalist group that became deeply opposed to mainstream Jewish teachings and lifestyle and splintered away from the Pharisaic government that had come to power in 76 BC. Considered by some to be pursuing an "adventuresome theology", it is also possible that this cult, or another similar organization, sprang from the Messianic Christian movement that, like the Essenes, subscribed to deeply apocalyptic beliefs and arose in the same remote area of Syrio-Palestine.

ESSENIC CULTURE

In common with many other cults, the Essenes' way of life included degrees of initiation, vows of poverty and celibacy, ritual meals and a form of purifying baptism. They rejected the more traditional Jewish sacrifices and dressed in white robes. Their community was strictly ordered, running along almost military lines. Their austere lifestyle arose out of the belief that the Day of Judgement, Armageddon, was imminent and that the cult members represented the ultimate generation to inhabit the Earth. In preparation for this terrible event they had elected to live a life of self-denial, and to distance themselves from the Sadducees, Pharisees, and Maccabees who were governing the land of Israel. This was in stark contrast to the prevailing social and sexual mores dictated through the Temple in Jerusalem. From the evidence of an extensive cemetery at the site, the community seems to have been comprised largely of men, and among the most prominent members of the sect may have been John the Baptist, who is known to have preached within a few miles of the cult's centre. Its inner society was almost certainly a male-only club and the Essene women were probably housed in separate quarters, limiting themselves to a contemplative life.

The leader of this monastic community would have been not only a civil administrator but also a teacher, and would have arbitrated in any disputes. When necessary, he would also have adjudicated in expelling members from the community, either for a temporary period or for life if their misdemeanour was deemed serious enough.

ESSENIC BELIEFS

The provenance of the Dead Sea Scrolls, discovered in 1947 in the Wadi of Qumran, where the cult headquarters seems to have been founded, has long been the subject of fierce academic debate. However, according to some scholars, they constitute part of the library of the Essene community. One of the more important texts is effectively a strategy of war and suggests a belief among the Essenes that in the final conflict they, the Sons of Light, would do battle against the Sons of Darkness. This suggests that they based some of their beliefs on the principles of Zoroastrianism. The text envisages, in considerable detail, three campaigns to be waged over a 40-year period. The first two campaigns would be against the desert neighbours of the Israelites and the final campaign, which would be conducted for 29 years, would be conducted against the remaining wicked peoples of the world. The Essene community also believed implicitly in the existence and significance of angels in their struggle as Champions of the Light. The Essene site at Qumran seems to have been abandoned in about AD 70 and its precious documents left to posterity in nearby caves, where they lay for more than 2,000 years.

"In the abode of light are the origins of truth and from the source of darkness are the origins of error. In the hand of the Prince of Lights is dominion over all the sons of righteousness... And in the hand of the Angel of Darkness is all dominion over the sons of error."

**The Manual of Discipline,
Qumran Manuscripts**

Above: Poussin's *Adoration of the Golden Calf*, 1633. Depicting the Israelite's worship of the bull during Moses's absence.

GNOSTICS AND OTHER CHRISTIAN CULTS

In the first two centuries after the Crucifixion, Christianity was very far from being a united sect and was, in reality, thoroughly faction-ridden, with diverse groups promoting a number of traditions and ideologies that were quite distinct from what is now regarded as the "True Faith".

Above: Catacombe di San Pancrazio under the basilica in Trastevere, Rome – home to Christian cults.

The Roman catacombs were used as much to keep these fringe groups from persecution by the orthodox elders of the Church as they were to preserve Christians from their more tolerant Roman masters, who by and large regarded them as another oddball club in an already sect-ridden society. The extent to which the fringe groups irritated the orthodox apostolic leaders came to light after the Council of Nicaea, which met in the spring of AD 325 to hammer out a mainstream policy document. This famous declaration became known as the Nicene Creed and in its original form the statement ended with an official condemnation of the fringe cults, asserting that "these the catholic and apostolic Church of God anathemizes".

THE NAG HAMMADI LIBRARY

Among these fringe cults were the Gnostics, about whom little would be known were it not for the extraordinary discovery, in December 1945, of the Nag Hammadi library. A set of 12 leather-bound codices was unearthed by two brothers who were digging for fertilizer at a cave in Upper Egypt, near the modern village of Nag Hammadi and close by the ancient site of a Pachomian monastery. These amazing volumes were almost destroyed by a peasant woman who, believing them to be worthless, started to use them as fuel to fire her bread oven. Even after their antiquity was understood, so inflammatory were the texts to the Christian Church that knowledge of their very existence was suppressed for decades.

The codices included tracts written by followers of Gnosis, Christians who essentially held a common view that the world had been produced in a flawed state and that the only way to rise above its fate and to find God was through knowledge generated within oneself, as opposed to the orthodox view that humanity needs a divine hand outside and beyond itself. The library also included many fine early Christian texts, such as the *Origin of the World* and the *Gospel of Thomas*, which were banned from inclusion in what came to be known as the New Testament on the grounds that they constituted heresy.

Very little is known of the rituals of the Gnostics, but it is beyond doubt that they suffered great persecution at the hands of other Christians and many were stoned to death or exiled. It seems clear that the 12 leather-bound volumes were buried there with great care, sealed in a pottery urn to be found by some future and more tolerant society. They are perhaps a small indication of the great legacy of excellent Christian minds that was condemned to extinction in the flames of a pedantry through which broad truth died under censorship. Had it not been for the courage of an unknown Pachomian monk – who presumably received the documents for safekeeping and buried them, at some risk to himself, deep in the Egyptian soil – we might never have learned the beliefs of the Gnostics.

HERETICS

The fringe Christian cults owed much of their existence to the fact that many intelligent Christians found the biblical creation story of Genesis to be short on logic. For them it simply did not hold water. One of the foremost Gnostics, Valentinus, founder of the cult of the Valentinians, proposed the subtle but heretical argument that the supreme creator was an indivisible unit and that the flawed creator-god of Israel was merely an inferior derivative. Another radical group, the Marcionites, believed that the god of Israel and the god who had generated Jesus Christ, one imperfect, the other perfect, were separate entities, since the Israelite god had brought into being a world filled with disease, pain and suffering while the Christian deity was a god of light and love.

"I am the first and the last. I am the honoured one and the scorned one. I am the wife and the virgin. I am the mother and the daughter ... I am the barren one and many are her sons ... why have you hated me in your counsels?"

Codex VI, Nag Hammadi

Among the most extreme cults were the Manichaeans, severe ascetics following the teachings of the Persian philosopher Mani. They survived as a sect in Europe until well into the Middle Ages, giving rise to the descriptive expression "manic".

Most of these early Christian cults proclaimed, in some form, the concept of dualism – two parallel but separate worlds, one characterized by light, spirituality and goodness; the other dark, material in nature and essentially flawed. From this basis, they argued that Christ could only have been a spiritual presence and never "made flesh", as he was clearly a product of the non-material world of light.

They had also moved away from the mainstream belief of a male God, envisaging a powerful female presence in the cosmos, the source of knowledge that the Greeks had called *Sophia*, beside whom the creator of the temporal world was a demi-god, characterized by envy and spite. It was these heretical notions that provided the excuse to persecute the cults. By AD 500, they had mostly disappeared. However, while they existed, they were a force of intellect and reason.

ATTIS AND CYBELE

In the long line of incestuous life and death tragedies that mark the fertility cults of the ancients, few can be more dramatic or bloody in its enactment than that of the Anatolian goddess, Cybele, and her ill-fated consort, Attis.

Their story developed in Phrygia – the ancient kingdom of the Anatolian plateau that reached its zenith about 800 years before the birth of Christ – and it presented a variation on stories known to the Sumerians and Babylonians of Mesopotamia. What makes the Phrygian cult unusually significant is that it is the vehicle by which the god and goddess came to Europe. Attis, the son of Agdistis and Nana and the Phrygian version of the Mesopotamian god Dumuzi, was believed, in common with his counterpart, to have been a shepherd king in the misty heroic age. In some versions of the myths, Cybele, the Queen of Heaven and goddess of life, was his incestuous mother, while in others he was conceived immaculately by Nana when she placed a ripe almond in her bosom.

Attis had to die to be reborn. In some legends he was gored by a wild boar, in others he castrated himself beneath the sacred tree of the goddess and bled to death. His corpse then became a pine tree and from the drops of his blood grew violets. Legend had it that his body would not decay until the time of his resurrection and that his father, Agdistis, founded a priestly cult in the city of Pessinus and inaugurated an annual festival to honour his son's name.

That the cult had come to Europe can be attributed to a curious piece of military strategy. The Roman legions were embroiled in a drawn-out campaign of attrition brought by the Carthaginian general, Hannibal. The oracles advised that if the sacred icon of the great Phrygian mother goddess – a jagged piece of black meteorite rock that resided in the cult centre at Pessinus near modern Ankara – was carried to Rome and installed in the Temple of Victory on the Palatine Hill, Rome would win the Second Punic War. The stone was entrusted to Roman ambassadors and, subsequently, Hannibal failed to win the day. He returned to Carthage, where he was defeated in 202 BC and forced to spend the rest of his life in exile.

THE DAY OF BLOOD

Though many of the old Near-Eastern cults relied on a dramatic reconstruction of the death of the fertility god, the Cybeline priests who accompanied the cult to Rome in about 204 BC re-enacted Attis's demise in a singularly horrific ritual, the annual Day of Blood, which took place on 24 March, three days into the Attis Festival. The priests of the goddess, the *galli*, were not ordinary men since they had been initiated into her service by a dreadful act of self-denial. In emulating the fate of Attis they performed a sacrifice that was far from symbolic, since each physically castrated himself before presenting his severed testicles to Cybele and burying them in the earth. Once these priests had emasculated themselves, they wore women's clothes and ornaments for the rest of their lives and each year, in the great rite, they gashed their limbs drawing fresh blood, a sacrifice to the goddess through the giving of their own life strength.

At the commencement of the Attis rite, a model of the god was attached to a pine tree. This was then garlanded with violets and strips of coloured wool before being paraded through the streets to the Temple of Cybele by an honoured Guild of Tree Bearers. By convention, the priests and the acolytes who lined the way wore white, the symbol not only of purity and innocence but also of death. To the casual observer it might have seemed an attractive vision, yet beside the road stood grimmer portents, scabbards holding knives and swords.

Slowly, the fervour of the bystanders grew to a frenzy while the priests in their oddly oriental and androgynous costumes processed with small Attis images hanging around their necks. Their chanting and drumming became mingled with more shrill notes as they gashed themselves repeatedly with knives and many of the bystanders, caught up in the hysteria, copied them with any instrument of mutilation they could lay their hands

Above: A Roman silver shield, depicting Attis and Cybele riding in a lion-drawn chariot.

upon. Some hacked off their own manhood and, with their life blood ebbing away and spattering the white costumes with scarlet colour, ran to the icon to dash their genitals against the black stone.

Three days after the Day of Blood, the Hilaria Festival commenced, which was preceded by an all-night candle-lit vigil culminating a sequence of events with such clear similarities to the Christian Easter rites that comparison cannot be avoided. The purpose of the Attis rites was to symbolize the cycle of nature. Attis had to die to be reborn and to inject new life into the soil, but was this also the precedent for much of that which became incorporated into the Gospels as the story of Passiontide?

The cult of Cybele, distinct from the Attis rites but clearly related to them, was generally orgiastic in nature and was served by other priests known as curetes or

> *"Man after man, his veins throbbing with the music, his eyes fascinated by the sight of the streaming blood, flung his garments from him, leaped forth with a shout, and seizing one of the swords which stood ready for the purpose, castrated himself on the spot. Then he ran through the city, holding the bloody pieces in his hand."*

***The Golden Bough*, James Frazer**

corybantes, taking their name from Corybas, one of the mythical sons of Cybele who supposedly introduced her rites into Phrygia. In spite of its violence and gore, the cult attracted numerous followers and voyeurs, surviving until fairly late on in the period of the Roman Empire.

ANCIENT ORGIASTIC CULTS

While some of the ancient cults placed emphasis on strict austerity and celibacy, and others incorporated a degree of sexuality necessary for the healthy observance of a fertility religion, a few went down a decidedly extreme path, pursuing principles of hedonism in which restraint was completely cast aside.

In the ancient Dionysian and Bacchanalian orgies the abandoning of propriety exceeded all bounds.

The Greek deity of wine and intoxication, Dionysus, was born the illegitimate son of Zeus, the Greek ruler of gods, and Semele, one of the many extra-marital liaisons of which Zeus's wife, Hera, took a decidedly jaundiced view. Semele met an untimely death while in the sixth month of her pregnancy, though not at the hands of Hera. Ironically,

she demanded that her lover show himself in his true form, but was then struck dead by the lightning bolts that emerged from the brilliance of his image. Zeus was then obliged to pluck the unborn foetus from her and insert it into his thigh; Dionysus was thus the "twice-born god". In a desire to destroy him, Hera introduced Dionysus to the delights of the vine before rendering him mad in his young adulthood. He was rehabilitated by the Phrygian mother goddess, Cybele, and his journeys took him to India, where he acquired an entourage of lusty satyrs and maenads before returning to Greece. Once there, he was determined to wreak havoc by introducing drunken orgies during which the participants, mostly women, were seized with uncontrollable, intoxicated frenzy and ecstasy. His death came amid great violence – he was said to have been ripped apart and consumed by the Titans.

DIONYSIAC CULTS

Membership of the Dionysiac cult involved stages of initiation and some of the best evidence for the rites is depicted on the walls of a first-century AD villa, excavated close to the ruins of Pompeii. These depict the lady of the house, seated, while a youth reads a liturgy before her and a girl brings offerings before the High Priestess, who is also present. In the cult festivals, including the *Anthesteria*, the *Agrionia* and the *Katagogia,* Dionysus is represented by a giant phallus, largely as a symbol of sexual arousal and without particular fertility connotations. The participants wore masks that identified them with the spirits of nature. On such occasions the party-goers were seriously intent on letting their hair down and shedding their inhibitions. The rites included mystery plays, not unlike those of the ancient Greek town of Eleusis, and part of the interest of the cult followers lay in the probability that the Dionysiac mystery plays would open a doorway to life after death. These mysteries constituted an important part of the religious beliefs of people living in Central and Southern Italy from the second century BC onward. Again, the frescos from the villa at Pompeii convey a vivid impression, including depictions of nature, divination, penitence, flagellation and impending ritual dismemberment. They are overseen by Dionysus and Ariadne, the vegetation goddess who, according to tradition, was seduced and then abandoned by Theseus on the island of Naxos.

FURTHER ORGIASTIC RITES

To the Dionysiac rites were added the Bacchanals of the Roman god, Bacchus, the so-called Orphic hymns, and the celebration of the Phrygian deity, Sabazios. These frenzied festivities spread throughout the Greco-Roman world. From the second century BC there is evidence that they were seen as a distinct threat to the rule of law imposed by the Senate, and their activities were curbed. This was only a temporary measure and toward the end of the Roman Empire their activities burgeoned again. Some of the Roman emperors, including Caligula and Hadrian, went so far as to have their images actually modelled on Dionysus.

By no means were all such activities orgiastic, as is evidenced from the records of one of the cultic societies. In April AD 176, the monthly assembly of the Iobacchi in Athens was supervized by a new high priest, one Herodes Atticus. During the meeting, a new set of society rules was formalized, speeches were delivered, wine was drunk, meat was eaten and a sacred drama was performed. This was merely a small official meeting at which members paid honours to the god amid comparative restraint. However, as with so many of the cults of the Classical era, the Dionysiac and Bacchanalian revels faded away as the empire collapsed.

Opposite: A first century AD glass cameo, depicting the initiation of Ariadne (Arianna) to the cult of Dionysus.

THE ELEUSINIAN MYSTERIES

The mystery cults, which enjoyed a popular following in many parts of the ancient world, were so-called because they combined ritual with a myth, the details of which were kept secret from all but an inner core of privileged initiates.

The most famous of these cults was that of Eleusis, in Greece, which was devoted to honouring the tragic myth of Demeter the Great Mother, her daughter Persephone and the mortal Prince Triptolemos. The cult attracted a sizeable priesthood of initiates, or *Eumolpids*, from among the upper social strata of the city. It would be a contradiction in terms if we knew the exact nature of the myth. Its secret has been well kept but it seems that, through the rites, a secret experience was transmitted to the devotees that glorified the death of the mortal body and ensured a happy and immaculate afterlife for the spirit. The process of initiation probably involved oath-taking against felonies such as killing and stealing and a general promise to live by a code of holiness and discipline.

HYMN TO DEMETER

In the beautifully wrought Homeric *Hymn to Demeter*, the youthful Persephone, daughter of Demeter, was gathering flowers in a meadow in company with the children of the god Oceanus when the ground opened up and Aidoneus (Hades), the god of the Underworld, caught her and swept her away to his kingdom. It was not until Hecate, the goddess of pathways, heard Persephone's cries that Demeter, the corn mother, was alerted. Distraught, she searched in vain for her daughter until Hecate delivered the dreadful news of Persephone's fate. In her grief she began to neglect the temporal world of nature until it shrivelled and died, while she mourned her loss at Eleusis in the guise of an aged crone. Concerned at the damage that was being wrought, Zeus sent the gods of Olympus, one by one, to rouse Demeter, but to no avail. The grieving goddess refused to return to her care until, at last, Zeus himself intervened and Aidoneus was persuaded to allow Persephone back to her mother. Alas, she had already tasted the pomegranate seed of death, which secured her to the Underworld, so

in a compromise negotiated by Zeus, she was allowed to return to the world of life for just one season each year. It was then that Demeter returned to her role as the mother of the Earth and showed herself to Triptolemos and the Eleusinian lords as an ear of corn.

THE KEY TO THE MYSTERIES

It was in this secret signal of Demeter's return that the key to the Eleusinian mysteries probably lay. This ritual drama was performed to ensure the continuing cycle of nature on the fertile Eleusinian plains left parched by the Mediterranean summer sun.

The Eleusinian Mysteries took place in the autumn of each year. On 19 September there was a great procession of worshippers from Athens to Eleusis. This procession was preceded by a proclamation of the rites, a baptism of regeneration in the sea and the sacrifice of pigs. A torch-lit restoration of Persephone to her mother then followed, taking place in the Great Hall of the Mysteries. A sacred marriage may also have been celebrated in which the High Priest, representing Zeus, and the High Priestess, playing the role of Demeter, performed a symbolic intercourse.

If this was the case then the indications are that the performance took place under the cover of darkness while the worshippers awaited an outcome on which they believed that their spiritual salvation rested. At the conclusion, and in what was undoubtedly the climax of the rites, the High Priest emerged in the glare of bright lights bearing an ear of corn. He proclaimed this to be the outcome of the mystical union – the embodiment of Demeter and of her child, and the sign of new life in the fields.

Opposite: Relief representing Triptoleme, the prince of Eleusis, between Demeter and Persephone, the Great Mother. Fifth century BC.

ROMAN RITES

The Eleusinian Mysteries were popular enough to have been celebrated by many of the Roman emperors from the time of Augustus, although some Roman leaders, including Emperor Nero, were barred from initiation. It is also known, from various inscriptions that have been discovered at Eleusis, that several Roman governors of the province were initiated and observed the rites with considerable dedication.

ARTEMIS AT EPHESUS

The cult of the goddess Artemis – the Greek counterpart of the Roman goddess Diana – who with her twin brother Apollo was one of the divine children of Zeus and the goddess Leto, possessed a strong mix of oriental and occidental traditions and existed at a variety of places in the ancient world, including Perga in Pamphylia, Antioch-near-Pisidia and Magnesia-on-the-Maeander.

In Rome, the imagery of Artemis was faithfully copied and she was provided with a magnificent sanctuary on the Aventine, where each year a great festival was held in her honour, while at Patras, in Achaea, her cult statue had been a gift from the Emperor Augustus. The worship of Artemis was extensive and reached as far as Egypt but no cult centre matched the fame of Ephesus, a city on the shores of the Aegean Sea.

According to Strabo, the Ephesus temple was torn down and rebuilt seven times but its most famous version was built in about the sixth century BC. It was considered to be one of the seven wonders of the ancient world, being not a great deal smaller than St Peter's Basilica in Rome and constructed of Phrygian marble inlaid with gold. According to Pliny, the Ionic roof was supported by 127 columns, each 19 metres (62 feet) high.

"I sing of Artemis, whose shafts are of gold, who cheers on the hounds, the pure maiden, shooter of stags, who delights in archery, own sister to Apollo with the golden sword. Over the shadowy hills and windy peaks she draws her golden bow, rejoicing in the chase and sends out grievous shafts. The tops of the high mountains tremble and the tangled wood echoes awesomely with the outcry of beasts; earth quakes and the sea also where fishes shoal."

From the Homeric Hymn to Artemis, translated by Evelyn-White

WORSHIPPING AT THE STATUE OF ARTEMIS

The great statue of Artemis at Ephesus is striking and provocative not least because of its many breasted appearance, which some have claimed also represents either ripe dates or even a kind of androgynous genitalia, but which in any event blossoms with an exuberant riot of life-giving essence. Each year, on 25 May, the statue of the goddess was carried in procession on a cart from the temple to the amphitheatre in the city centre, where it was greeted ecstatically by a crowd assessed to have numbered as many as 30,000 pilgrims. The processional route, a distance of a mile, had been covered from the weather with a marble colonnade, built at huge expense by a wealthy Roman patron.

In the comparable Roman festival, a vast and splendid procession carried her votary priestesses to the temple on a cart pulled by deer, the sacred animal of Artemis. There a sacred pyre was built around the altar and surrounded by a barrier of wet green logs. Onto it were placed sacrificial offerings of live animals and harvest fruits. Beasts as large as bears are claimed to have been dragged to the altar, chained there and burnt to death.

The precise details of other rites that took place in Artemis's honour are vague, but the Scottish writer and anthropologist, James Frazer, describes a ceremony that took place each year in the Arcadian region at Condylea, when an effigy of Artemis was hanged in her sacred grove. Similar traditions of hanging exist elsewhere. At Melite, in Phthia, a young woman was said to have hung herself. Her corpse vanished but her image appeared beside that of Artemis. A woman also hung herself at Ephesus and was taken by the goddess, dressed in the clothes of a deity and called Hecate. Sometimes it would seem that animals such as goats were hung sacrificially each year to honour the goddess.

Elsewhere, the Greek writer Pausanias recorded the strange story surrounding the origin of Sparta's Artemis statue. In a brutal yearly rite, the children of Sparta were beaten before the sculpture until they bled.

The Artemis statue was taken to Sparta from Tauris by Orestes and Iphigenia, but had then been lost for many years. It was rediscovered by two children, Astrabacus and Alopecus, who were the grandsons of Amphisthenes. In what seems a divinely unjust punishment for having set eyes on the sacred image, they were consigned to a horrible fate – insanity.

Artemis was the mistress of the natural world, on the one hand seen as a virgin huntress while on the other, a bountiful and fertile mother. Like other fertility goddesses, including the Phrygian Cybele and the Syrian Astarte, she was ministered to not only by priestesses but also, chiefly, by a priesthood. At the head of the priesthood stood the High Priest or Megabysos, who was a eunuch, self-castrated as part of his crazed devotion. The priestly caste within the temple confines, which numbered several hundreds, also included curetes and acrobats. The former were responsible for creating a bedlam of noise when the birth of Artemis was celebrated in order that Hera, the jealous wife of Zeus, would not hear the cries of her philandering husband's illegitimate daughter. The acrobats allegedly walked about on their toes and were involved in the ritual dancing.

In a precedent of Christian customs, the temple area at Ephesus was ordained as a safe haven for certain types of criminal in what was known as the Asyl right. At first the Asyl rights were quite limited, but they were enlarged under Alexander the Great and subsequently still further by both Mithradates and the Roman emperor, Marcus Antonius. Although attempts were made by subsequent emperors to curb the Asyl rights, they remained in force until the close of the empire.

Opposite: The statue of Belle Artemis from Ephesus, second century AD.

THE CULT OF
THE BULL

Since the time of the Stone-Age portraits in the great European painted caverns, the bull has ranked with the bear, the elephant and the lion as an enduring symbol of virility and strength, and so bull cults have attracted almost as many forms as devotees.

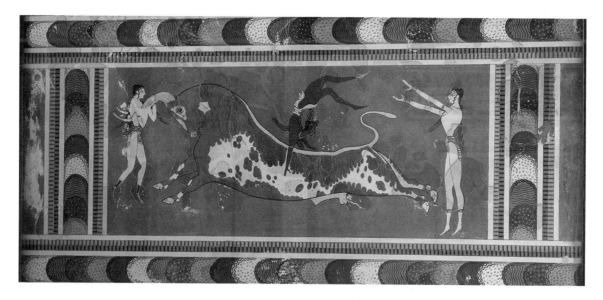

Above: The Toreador Fresco, c.1450 BC, Greece. A person leaps over a bull during ritual games.

Their Palaeolithic ancestors march across the ceiling of the Great Hall of Lascaux; as hybrids they have guarded the gateways to fabled cities such as Nineveh and Kalakh; and they appear unstintingly in the faiths of Egyptians, Persians and Hindus.

The mystery cults of Attis and Cybele were among the many that included aspects of bull worship in variations of a ritual known as the taurobolium, in which a bull was probably not merely sacrificed but subjected to some form of game. The game went on for several days, with similarities to a western rodeo, and may have evolved into the present-day spectacle of bull-fighting.

The Roman writer Prudentius, in the fourth century AD, details that as part of the less public bull ritual through which the initiates passed, a novice was placed in a ceremonial pit, the roof of which was covered with a wooden grating. A bull, spectacularly adorned with gold and other finery, was led to stand over the pit and its

throat was cut with a ritual instrument so that the bull's blood gushed into the pit and over the worshipper in a bizarre form of baptism, purification and renewal. Those initiated in this manner were either considered to be baptized for life or to need renewal of their purification after a period of years.

The slaughter of the bull also reflected the violent death and subsequent resurrection that characterized other gods of fertility and vegetation. Like Attis, Dionysus was believed to have met a bloody fate, being ripped apart and cannibalized by the Titans, who were responding to the command of the goddess Hera. She was bitterly jealous of Dionysus, who was born from the thigh of Zeus, and engineered his death as revenge for her husband's philandering. In Crete, his death was remembered in a savage ritual, which climaxed with a live bull being torn to pieces by worshippers and parts of it, including the heart, eaten. Bull's testicles became a prized cultic offering and the practice was sometimes taken to extreme lengths. It is reported that, in AD 160, a devotee named Carpus carried a pair of bull testicles from the Vatican Hill in Rome to Lyons in Gaul so that he could present them at the temple of Cybele.

THE MINOTAUR

The most celebrated focus of the bull cult undoubtedly rested at Knossos, in Crete, where according to Greek myth, the Minotaur – the hybrid monster born to Pasiphae in retribution for King Minos's failure to sacrifice bulls to the god Poseidon – roamed in its labyrinth. The ruins of the royal palace at Knossos still bear testimony to the veneration of the bull in the "Horn of Consecration" motifs and in sculptures that are the peculiar hallmark of Cretan holy places. The Minoans in Crete probably copied the Attis cult and passed it on to the Mycenaeans in mainland Greece.

Although the bull was a beast of the Earth it was also very often envisaged as being the incarnate representative of the god of the Sun or Moon in what were essentially cults of solar or lunar worship. According to James Frazer, the Cretan kings were either actually or symbolically slaughtered at the end of their fixed term of office – a period of eight years representing the solar cycle of the planet Venus – in a pattern of renewal that reflected not only the fate of the dying and rising gods of nature but the passage of more heavenly bodies. It was in this connection that the tribute of seven youths and seven maidens was sent to Knossos by the Athenians. Their deaths were seen as a "scapegoat" for King Minos and as a means of renewing his divine energy for a further eight years. Tradition has it that the victims were locked in the labyrinth with the Minotaur to await their fate. Other reports suggest that they may have been roasted alive in a bronze vessel fashioned in the shape of a bull's head or of a bull-headed man.

"The bellowing bull, freely flowing with luscious drops, places his seed in the plants as an embryo. He shatters the trees and slaughters the demons; he strikes terror into every creature with his enormous deadly weapon. Even the sinless man gives way before the god bursting with seed like a bull, when the thundering Parjanya slaughters those who do evil."

The Hymns of the Rig Veda

RELATED CULTS

Knossos essentially reflects a solar worshipping cult and although the Minotaur received its notoriety through the writings of various classical authors – including Hesiod, Homer and Plutarch, and through the exploits of the Athenian hero, Theseus, rescuer of Ariadne – it may in reality have been little more than an image, a bronze figure with the body of a man and the head of a bull, symbolizing the power of the Sun.

In the area of Europe north of the Alps, the Celts worshipped a three-horned bull god called Tarvos Trigaranos, but it also seems likely that the pagan horse-sacrificing cults of the North European races were an adaptation of the early Mediterranean bull cults. The twelfth-century writer Giraldus Cambrensis later reported a rite performed by the Ulster tribes for the coronation of the Irish kings that has familiar echoes. During the ritual, a mare was killed, dismembered and boiled. The monarch then bathed in the resulting broth and ate parts of the flesh. The bull cults effectively died out in the fourth century AD when the Christianized Roman emperors, including Theodosius and Constantine the Great, banned human and animal sacrifice throughout the empire.

MITHRAISM

This cult, seemingly in contradiction of its name, was devoted to the Persian god of light, Ahura Mazda, to whom Mithras was the chief attendant. Thus, among the statuary of the Mithraeum at Santa Prisca in Rome, Ahura Mazda is thought to be the unnamed reclining figure beside whom Mithras stands not only in service but also as the intercessor between the god and mortal Earth.

Known to the Persians as Mithra, he became Mithras only in the Roman cult that existed until about AD 200 and which arose out of the older Persian Zoroastrianism.

According to myth, Mithras, the apotheosis of truth, was born from a rock. His first task involved a titanic struggle with another of Ahura Mazda's creations, a wild bull. He subdued the bull but was then obliged to slit its throat and from its blood sprang all the plant life on Earth. This was a popular theme of classical sculpture, which depicted Mithras standing astride the bull and plunging his weapon into its neck. His chief adversary, though, was to be Ahriman, the lord of darkness, who attempted to destroy the world by flood.

THE SPREAD OF MITHRAISM
The cult was perhaps an indication of the burgeoning interest in Sun worship. It was never popular with the civilian population of the Roman Empire, but its membership spread, particularly in the east, among the military under Emperor Flavius. In the western arm of the empire it tended to be confined to frontier outposts. In AD 307, under Diocletian, a sanctuary was built on the River Danube and dedicated to Mithras in an effort to sustain the flagging military power of the legions, but under Gratian, the Mithraic temples were eventually closed down in AD 377. Around Europe the relics of a number of Mithraic temples have survived and at Walbrook, in England, there exists the remains of a fine Mithraeum.

BELIEF AND RITUAL
The details of Mithraic belief and ritual have largely been shrouded, although an Egyptian magical papyrus dating from about AD 300 appears to offer some details of invocations and initiations. Mithraism was concerned with dark and light, the rising and the setting of the Sun, birth and death, in which respect two of its heavenly

"When he had reached his cave, a raven sent by the Sun brought the saviour word that the moment of sacrifice had arrived, and, Seizing his victim by the nostrils, he plunged the knife into its flank. Wheat sprang from the bull's spinal cord and from its blood the vine – whence the bread and wine of the sacramental meal."

The Masks of God, Joseph Campbell

"officers" played a strong role. One, Cautes, always portrayed carrying an upright flaming torch, stands for the powers of good, light, spring and birth; the other, Cautopates, carries his torch inverted and represents evil, darkness, winter and death. The cult was built very much in the style of a mystery religion in which the immortal soul was perceived to travel on an endless journey during which its time on Earth was merely a temporary trial. The mysteries were focused equally on death and the rebirth of the soul, an interest that would have found sympathy among the soldiers of the legions for whom mortality was especially precarious. At birth, the soul was believed to descend from the light and receive the seven "sins". It was then at liberty to free itself from taint during life and to ascend back into the light in a spiritual rebirth so that it was judged, at death, on personal merit. Its possession would be contested between angels and devils, with Mithras taking the role of judge. Even if it was to pass the arbitration of Mithras, its ordeal was still far from over since it then had to win various tests brought by "Customs Officials" before reaching its goal.

Mithraic temples were built underground and were

Above: Mithras slaying the bull in the Antiquario Communale, Rome.

referred to as "caves". Membership was restricted to men, though their fraternity found parallels in the sororities of the cult of Cybele. The seven grades of initiation through which noviciates passed on the stairway to absolution included tests of physical and mental endurance and of abstinence. These grades began in the lower or Servitor levels with the title of Raven, ascending through Bridegroom and Soldier. In the Senior or Participant grades, initiates commenced at the level of Lion followed by Persian, Courier of the Sun and Father. At each level the initiation rituals varied.

A sacred fire representing the Sun and light was kept burning in the underground Mithraic sanctuaries, and ceremonies re-enacting the myth were accompanied by fireworks and lights reflected in water and, possibly, by moving images.

The cult of Mithras was, however, never large. It was always a private form of worship with a small membership of dedicated men and did not have the impact on Classical Rome that has sometimes been suggested.

THE DEATH CULTS OF MEXICO

The violent and often bloody religious cults that marked much of Mexico's pre-Hispanic history are difficult to piece together in detail, not least because the Conquistadors did such a thorough job of destroying the earlier cultural records.

Mexico tends to be identified popularly with the Aztecs, but they were only the last of a series of civilizations that began with the Olmecs and continued through the Zapotecs, the Toltecs and others. The Mayans, who bordered on Mexico in the Yucatán Peninsula and Central America, represented a separate civilization.

The mythology of the gods of the Central American cultures was, in itself, intensely violent. Tezcatlipoca, the Sun god of the Aztecs, was believed to have dragged the Earth mother, Cipactli, from the primeval waters in a ferocious creation battle, during which she bit off his left foot and he tore out her lower jaw. In a similarly brutal vein, the tutelary war god, Huitzilpochtli, sprang from the belly of his decapitated mother, Coatlicue, and immediately slaughtered his sister and 400 brothers in retribution for her death.

EVIDENCE OF HUMAN SACRIFICE

From very early times there seems to have been a cultic interest in human sacrifice. The ancient gods of Mexico had a distinct appetite for blood, which was believed to cool their own fiery veins and tempers. In caves in the Tehuacán valley, a little more than 100 miles southeast of Mexico City, evidence of decapitated skeletons with their heads smashed and deposited in baskets suggests rites of this kind existed as early as 7000 BC.

Some of the most dramatic pictorial evidence comes from Veracruz where, in the Classical period that extended from AD 150 to AD 900, a horrific ball game was played. At El Tajin, there existed football pitches on which the final accolade was not to receive a ornamental victor's cup or plate, but to take the life of the losing captain by ripping out his heart with a flint knife. The game was refereed by the god of death – who is depicted in stone reliefs by a skull and skeleton.

RITUAL KILLING

The Toltec era also saw some gruesome individual excesses – private residences contained sacrificial altars in their courtyards from which evidence has come to light of ritual slaughter and cannibalization of bodies – but it was the Zapotecs of the Post-Classical period who indulged in some of the most appalling practices. Ruled effectively by a High Priest at Mitla, the "City of the Dead" in the valley of Oaxaca, the Zapotec cult regularly took captives of war, kings and commoners alike, and ripped out their hearts as offerings to the gods. For these rites a whole paraphernalia was reserved, including sacrificial knives and vessels to receive organs and blood. It was also common practice that when a king or ruler died he was accompanied in death by his wives, doctors and full domestic retinue, all of whom were slain to keep him in the manner to which he had become accustomed when he reached the land of the dead.

AZTEC SAVAGERY

Of all the South and Central American races, the Aztecs gained the most notoriety for their blood-thirsty festivities, perhaps because they were the most closely observed but also because they were the most successful militarists and, therefore, in a position to obtain large numbers of suitable victims. Their strategy in battle was to capture as many of the enemy as possible, who were then transported and sacrificially slaughtered at the hands of the awesome cultic priests. Their gods, like those of the Zapotecs, were not satisfied unless served constantly with human blood and, in particular, human hearts. Thus, the great Aztec sun god, Tezcatlipoca, received a bizarre annual sacrifice. A captive warrior was accorded the honour of representing the god for a year, during which he lived in luxury with all that he required but, at the end of his time of office, he was escorted to

the temple, where he mounted the steps, was laid on the altar and had a ceremonial obsidian knife plunged into his chest. Likewise, the warrior sun god, Huitzilopochtli, required human blood and hearts to give him sufficient energy to rise from the underworld each morning and begin his traverse of the sky.

On Earth, the rain god, Tlaloc, would not bring the summer drought to a close without the mass sacrifice of children on sacred mountain altars, and the god of vegetation, Xipe Totec, demanded that his priests wore the skin of flayed captives for 21 days, until it rotted away.

An insight into the Aztec religious mentality can be found in the records of a ritual slaughter, in 1323, of a princess of the Colhuacan people who was given to the Aztecs as a bridal gift for their king. The priests sacrificed her in the belief that she would become a war goddess. Yet in this is revealed an implicit belief that he or she who

Above: Priests cutting out the heart of a youth to sacrifice to the sun. From the Aztec Codex, sixteenth century, Mexico.

had died under the sacrificial knife, and whose heart had been torn from their breast so brutally, was destined not for the dark Land of the Dead but for the Paradise of the Gods, where they would spend an idyllic eternity. Each deity would thus take and preserve his own.

A telling epitaph to this exceptionally gruesome chapter of human religious expression occurred during the reign of Ahuitzotl (1486–1502), the predecessor of the last ill-fated ruler of the Aztecs, Motecuhzoma Xocoyotzin. Records show that, in 1487, no less than 20,000 captives were sacrificed during the dedication of the Great Temple of Tenochtitlan, where Mexico City now stands, their heads impaled on a seemingly endless skull-rack.

THE CELTIC DRUIDS

The Celtic star arose somewhere in the upper reaches of the Danube, perhaps Switzerland or Austria, in about the seventh century BC among a central European people who only reached the British Isles late in their time.

If they possessed an overriding weakness, one which led eventually to their downfall, it was that they were governed by a religious cultic hierarchy, the Celtic Druid priesthood. Remarkably little is actually known about the priesthood because the Celtic Druids were the guardians of a complex and sophisticated religion that they were unable to preserve other than by word of mouth. Much of the popular fallacy about the Celtic Druids has come about because they have been victims of an almost unparalleled level of romance and distortion that portrays them as wearing long bushy beards and white nighties, and stamping round Stonehenge waving golden sickles and bits of mistletoe.

In reality, our understanding of the cult of Celtic Druidry is gleaned through the limited, and often second-hand, observations of classical writers such as Diodorus Siculus, Julius Caesar and Strabo, who were copying the now lost works of Posidonius, and through fragments of archaeology. There is also a limited amount of Irish Celtic literature, of which the best known is probably the Ulster Cycle.

We can be certain that the Celtic Druids rarely built permanent temples, although they may have used simple wooden structures, the evidence for which has been lost. Their favoured places of worship were clearings or groves in the oak forests called nemetons – sites which frequently developed an unsavoury reputation with the Roman empire builders.

Whether the Roman writer Lucan ever actually visited Marseilles is uncertain, and his depiction is unquestionably lurid. He does, nonetheless, accurately depict the kind of woodland clearings, often near springs, that the Celtic Druids favoured. Not only were the woods sacred to them but they also revered and made offerings to individual trees.

Above: A wicker man, containing its sacrificial victims.

DRUIDIC RITUAL

As far as the Celtic Druid priesthood went, little is known about it, although beyond doubt they represented a formidable religious force and were accomplished magicians. There is some suggestion that they wore gold chains bearing Sun and Moon symbols and that they carried sceptres. They may also have worn masks during ritual. Beyond this, much of our impression of Celtic Druids "at work"' is gained through a brief insight reported by the Roman writer Pliny, who described an activity that took place on the sixth day of the Moon's cycle.

The Celtic Druids performed human sacrifice, though with what frequency it is impossible to ascertain. Julius Caesar reported the horrific practice of burning victims alive in wicker cages that were perhaps sometimes fashioned to represent the human colossi popularized in the cult film, *The Wicker Man*. His commentary, however, has to be read with caution because he frequently wrote with a propagandist slant and at second hand.

The Celtic Druids seem to have regularly drowned victims and this particular style of ritualized slaughter is apparently depicted on the so-called Gundestrup Bowl, the superb Cimbrian silver cauldron recovered from a bog at Ravemøsen in Denmark. In all events, their desire for human sacrifice was primarily for the purposes of divination. There are descriptions of how they would, for example, stab or impale victims and predict future events from the manner of the death throes. The Celtic Druids also placed great emphasis on human heads, which were collected in battle and preserved in special niches in their sanctuaries – perhaps in the belief that within the skull lay an unquenchable repository of supernatural power.

It seems that various animals were sacred to the Celtic Druids, including the stag and the boar, which are often depicted in their religious art, but of their gods little can be revealed with any degree of certainty. Much of the romance attached to such figures as Dagda, Maeve, Nuada, Lugh, Gobniu and others has been manipulated and apparently degraded by clerical Christian writers whose interest has lain in making them objects of pagan boorishness and ridicule.

THE DECLINE OF THE CELTS

Probably too much of the sovereign power of the Celts lay in the cult of the Celtic Druids and it was an Achilles's heel that eventually brought them down. No government in history with an administration based on clerical rather than secular logic has survived the test of time because such regimes are invariably fuelled by fanaticism and intolerance and thus fail against outside worldly pressures.

THE WEAKNESS OF THE CELTS

A grove there was, untouched by men's hands from ancient times whose interlacing boughs enclosed a space of darkness and cold shade, and banished the sunlight from above. No rural Pan dwelt there, nor Sylvanus, ruler of the woods, no nymphs; but gods were worshipped there with savage rites, the altars were heaped with hideous offerings, and every tree was sprinkled with human gore. On these boughs, if antiquity, reverential of the gods, deserves any credit, birds feared to perch; in those coverts wild beasts would not lie down; no wind ever bore down upon that wood, nor thunderbolt hurled from black clouds; the trees, even when they spread their leaves to no breeze, rustled among themselves. Water also fell there in abundance from dark springs. The images of the gods, grim and rude, were uncouth blocks formed of felled tree-trunks.

(Pharsalia I, Lucan)

RADICAL

The American writer and journalist, Tom Wolfe, wrote that a cult is a religion with no political power, but he misunderstood the nature of the organism. In reality, little could be further from the truth. Cults wield very considerable power. Nine centuries ago the Catharists were threatening the entire political stability of southern France, and theirs was not an isolated example from history. In modern twentieth-century Japan, the Soka Gakkai cult claims a worldwide membership of 10 million and is merely the largest of 180,000 registered sects in a country that lost its national religious identity at the end of World War II when its emperor, perceived by millions to be a living God, was forced to announce capitulation over the radio.

The Unification Church of the Moonies owns a multi-billion dollar business empire in America and voices openly global ambitions. Sometimes these cults practice a genuinely austere and disciplined lifestyle but, more often than not, that which begins with good intention fails somewhere along the way. Religious fundamentalism and a simple communal life frequently translates as cash in the bank and a luxury ride for the cult. The cults described here represent only the tip of the iceberg. There are many thousands worldwide that, as often as not, trap their converts on a spiralling downward path that takes each disciple ever further from reality and the outside world.

THE CHRISTIAN RADICALS

For some three centuries after the end of the eighth century AD the heretical cults within the Christian movement took a back seat, but they were to re-emerge under different colours in the twelfth century.

The Orthodox Church had become weak and open to serious criticism among an illiterate and largely impoverished population. They attended services that were conducted in Latin and were therefore incomprehensible to many. They saw the clergy living in luxurious surroundings and supporting concubines and generally began to regard the Church establishment as corrupt. As a result of this, Christian cults built from among their own began to prove more attractive. The Church viewed this with considerable alarm, anticipating a direct threat to its ecclesiastical, theological and political power, and it responded with the enormous muscle that it had at its disposal. Among the earliest of the heretical sects that came to irritate the Christian establishment were the Waldensians and the Catharists.

THE WALDENSIANS

Founded in 1176 by Peter Waldo, an affluent merchant in the French city of Lyons, the Waldensians were given dispensation to preach by Pope Alexander III on the proviso that they obtained a licence from their local bishop. Their approach was deemed unacceptable, however, and their licence was withheld. They were subsequently excommunicated in 1184. Thus, the Waldensian heresy came into being since its followers, a band of itinerant and largely illiterate clergy, disagreed with the basic ritual, although not at first with the general doctrine, of Roman Catholicism. In later years they did, however, throw out the notions of purgatory, transubstantiation and the invocation of saints. Of the Orthodox services, they observed only baptism, marriage and the Eucharist, which were celebrated annually on Maundy Thursday. Against this they abandoned the formal confession of sins, rejected the Requiem Mass, excommunication, absolution, penance and payment of indulgences. While they claimed no ordained priesthood,

they practiced as evangelical ascetics but also brought women into their ministry, in itself a profound Catholic sacrilege. They also made translations of the New Testament and parts of the Old into more idiomatic language in an effort to make them more accessible.

While they were in no sense the pioneers of the Reformation, the Waldensians were, effectively, a Protestant religious sect. At the start they were active through much of the South of France and Lombardy, but their cells extended to Germany and Italy in the decades after the death of Waldo. In 1208, in an effort to reduce the undoubted popularity of the Waldensians, Pope Innocent III formed the Poor Catholics. Their role was to ape Waldensian practices that were within the remit of canonical law. By the middle of the thirteenth century, however, many of the Waldensians were imprisoned and those who were not burned as heretics were forced to flee to remoter regions of the Italian Alps, where their remnants survived. In the sixteenth century, they formed a predictable but loose alliance with the Calvinists and suffered intermittent persecution at the hands of the Catholic Church until the seventeenth century. Waldensians still exist in the North Italian region of Piedmont.

THE CATHARISTS

Although the Waldensians received their share of persecution, among the heretical sects it was the Catharists who came in for the full might of the Inquisitors' wrath. The term Cathari means the "pure ones" and the cult attracted large parts of the population of southern France before it spread to Italy, Spain and Flanders. It was the Catharists – or Albigenses – who effectively took up the banner of the earlier Gnostic sects like the Manichaeans. They believed in the principles of dualism – worlds of light and dark, good and bad, of which the material world was definitely on the dark side

Left: Waldensians worshipping the devil in the form of a goat. From Tinctoris's *Contra sectam Valdensium*, c.1460.

and in which Jesus Christ was never made flesh. Thus, the Crucifixion never took place and, for them, the cross held no significance. Nor did they worship in church buildings. They perceived the human soul as being trapped within a corrupt frame, the demands of which had to be suppressed. Leading on from this, predictably, they were against procreation of the flesh and marriage was frowned upon.

In their cultic activities they recognized two tiers of membership. One tier, the Perfect, had accepted a life of abstinence, celibacy and poverty and were comprised of Majors and Presbyters. The other tier, the Believers, made up the lay congregation and were probably no more than Catholics who had become disenchanted with the luxurious and out-of-touch lifestyles of the Orthodox clergy.

Persecution of the Catharists was launched on a horrific scale in 1208, following the assassination of a papal legate in Toulouse. This was identified as a Catharist conspiracy and a Crusade was mounted against them, headed by Simon de Montfort.

Some 200,000 zealots embarked upon a 20-year campaign of attrition, funded by the Catholic Church, during which large parts of southern France were laid waste. Essentially, their movement had become too large and too popular to be tolerated. In one dreadful reprisal the entire population of the town of Béziers was slaughtered. However, it was the assassination of the papal legate in Toulouse that, more than any other, catalyzed the establishment and the machinery of the Inquisition, which was established between 1227 and 1235. Those of the Catharists who were lucky enough to be left alive fled to the Balkans. They continued until the fifteenth century, after which the majority were slowly absorbed into the Muslim faith.

VOODOO

Not so much a radical religion as a blending of traditional West African beliefs with the Roman Catholic Church, voodoo became the rallying impetus of the slaves transported to the New World in the seventeenth century. It has been at its most active in Haiti, where the worst excesses of the plantation owners took place.

Today, Voodoo is practised worldwide, claiming over 40 million followers, but in past centuries it played an essential role in enabling transported slaves to identify with their country of origin and to develop a common language of faith and resistance. For this reason, and the accompanying fear of insurrection among the slave population, for many decades any person in Haiti caught possessing the trappings of Voodoo was imprisoned, tortured and executed.

VOODOO AND THE SLAVES' REVOLT

The religion, much distorted by imaginative writers and film producers, centres on the invocation of ancestral and other spirits, known as *loa*, which are called upon to enter the bodies of worshippers with good or evil intent. Those of a malevolent disposition may also be exorcized. Priests known as *houngans* or *manbos* act as the intercessors between the human and spirit worlds and exercise very considerable power over their congregation.

In the seventeenth century, Voodoo devotees who escaped from the slavers in Haiti and set up a precarious resistance movement in the hinterland were known as *maroons*, and were responsible, fighting under their leader, François Mackandal, for the first Slave Rebellion of 1758. The successor to Mackandal, Bookman, framed the infamous Voodoo Declaration of Independence, which includes, among other things, the statement, "Our gods who created the Sun which gives us light, who raised the waves and ruled the storm, they see all that the white man does… Our gods order us to avenge our wrongs."

That vengeance took shape in the final retribution against the Spanish plantation owners, led by Toussaint-L'Ouverture in 1802. Although he was captured and sent to France, where he was tried and executed by burning at the stake, the revolt effectively liberated Haiti from colonial rule. Voodoo spread across America and, although obliged to rest uneasily beside Roman Catholicism, it remained the dominant religion of Haiti, where it continued to be applied as a political tool. During the reign of Papa Doc Duvalier, Voodoo was employed as an effective form of terror tactic to control the population. Voodoo priests were included among the ranks of government and the infamous death squads, better known as the *Tonton Macoutes*.

The primitive animistic belief of the ancient African tribes from which Voodoo sprang is clear. The notion of a single god occupying the heavens is replaced by the belief that God is everywhere, in the animate and the inanimate and in the dead as well as the living. The religion thus employs large numbers of fetishes that include all manner of things, among them dog skulls, bones and chicken feathers. It also regularly involves snakes in its rituals and resorts to sacrifice as a means of expelling dangerous loa.

THE LIVING DEAD

Although one of the most notorious and colourful elements of Voodoo has been the Zombie, the concept of this "living dead" creature from whom the human soul has been separated away has been greatly romanticized and distorted. In reality, worshippers of Voodoo believe that when the human spirit has committed evil deeds during its temporal existence, it can be placed in a permanent state of nothing – in Christian terms, purgatory – as punishment. It is thus not the casual encounter with a Zombie that strikes fear into the hearts of believers, but the terror of becoming one in retribution for crimes.

Since a zombified state can, it is understood, be achieved through sorcery, the priesthood is able to command immense control and respect. Research has indicated that Voodoo priests do, indeed, have secret recipes for potions that can induce a catatonic near-death state. The power of most of these concoctions lies in a paralysing nerve toxin known to be synthesized in the flesh of certain Caribbean inshore fish.

OCCULT RITES

Notwithstanding the adverse publicity to which Voodoo priests have been subjected, they act most commonly for good, conducting exorcisms and administering healing rituals where conventional medicine has failed. These occult rites may involve the utterance of spells, drumming and dancing, use of herbal potions and the sacrifice of an animal, the most favoured being a black cockerel. While still alive, the cockerel's blood is applied to the subject and the spirit afflicting the patient is drawn by magical means into the bird, which is then tossed into a fire so that the malevolent influence is eliminated through the purifying action of the flames.

Voodoo is essentially an earth cult and the black virgin goddess, Erzulia, takes prominence in worship, though, in the United States, many of the Voodoo spirits have joined forces and identities with Christian saints. But Voodoo is also fundamentally a cult of ancestor worship and thus cemeteries and other places of burial take on great importance. It is in this context that the terrifying figure of Baron Samedi, the caretaker of the dead who rises from the ground in his top hat and black cloak, has achieved such colourful prominence in the celluloid world of Hollywood. In Cuba, a variation of the cult, known as Santeria, spread to the exile community in Miami toward the end of the 1990s. Since then it has become well established in Puerto Rico and offers an active website. It claims to practise neither "black" nor "evil magic".

Opposite: A voodoo festival by the waterfall of Saut d'Eau, Haiti.

THE KNIGHTS TEMPLAR

During the Middle Ages a number of Christian military and quasi-military fraternities sprang up, some of which were restricted to members possessing the rank of knight. Among them were the Knights Templar, derived from the Order of St John, which had been founded to care for the sick in Jerusalem, newly liberated from the Saracens.

Membership of the Templars required military service against the Saracens, who were still threatening Jerusalem with Muslim conquest. The Order – founded in Jerusalem in 1119 and officially licensed by Pope Honorius I in 1128 – played an active part in the Crusades, built its churches in an unusual and distinctive circular style and demanded of its brotherhood vows of fraternity, chastity and poverty. In requiring of its membership that they hand over their worldly possessions, the fraternity

amassed vast corporate wealth. Because of the affluence of the Order, and its developing role as international bankers and property dealers, it incurred considerable hostility from both Church and State, at times being accused of heresy, homosexuality and idolatry. By 1308, pressure was being exerted on Edward II to seize Templar property in England, Scotland and Ireland. His receipts of revenue were severely depleted in the baronial unrest that marked the early part of the fourteenth century and so Edward gave in to this pressure. The London Temple, headquarters of the Knights Templar in England, was closed and arrests began. The antagonism throughout Europe reached a climax in 1312, when Philip IV of France coerced Pope Clement V to suppress the Order. In the British Isles and on the Continent its members were incarcerated and many were tortured at the hands of the Papal Inquisition in an effort to extract bogus confessions. The Templars were thus effectively eradicated and most of their senior members executed. It was decreed that the Knights of St John of Jerusalem – who undertook charitable as well as military duties and whose membership included nursing nuns – should take over much of the property of the Templars, though this property was also to provide continuing secular benefit. The dowry of Isabella of France, at the time of her marriage to the English King Edward II, was derived largely from Templar riches, and the revenue of the English crown was replenished on a comparable scale of magnitude from the sale of Templar lands.

THE ROSICRUCIANS

On very similar lines to the Templars, but strictly non-militaristic, was the fraternal order known as the Rosicrucians. Their origins are founded largely in the myth of Christian Rosenkreutz who, it is claimed, lived between 1378 and 1484 as a member of the German aristocracy. Legend tells that, having visited Damascus and other Christian sites in the Near East, and gained a knowledge of alchemy, he founded his occult order somewhere in Germany. Following his death, the fraternity lay dormant until 1614 when the anti-Catholic paper, *Fama Fraternitas*, published a claim that the tomb of Christian Rosenkreutz, containing an uncorrupted cadaver, had been discovered. This stimulated the revival of the cult in Europe and it also attracted strong interest in England, particularly during the Puritan years of the Interregnum, when it was criticized heavily by the Church for "turning divinity into fantasy". Although the English following continued, and

many of the occult texts were translated and published, it was not until the end of the nineteenth century that a formal fraternity was inaugurated, taking the title Societa Rosicruciana in Anglia (SRIA).

THE SRIA

Founded by the freemason, Robert Wentworth Little, with the collaboration of fellow masons, the SRIA was launched in 1865 in association with its German parent society. It attracted many within freemasonry from which the grade of Master Mason was an essential prerequisite for membership. Its charter was based on grades and rituals that supposedly dated from medieval times, though they were probably copied from a text of no greater antiquity than 1781. There is, incidentally, a Masonic degree known as the Rose-Croix Eighteenth Degree, which, it is claimed by some historians, was derived from principles of Rosicrucianism and was worked in England as an independent discipline of the Masons under Sir Thomas Dunckerley from about the end of the eighteenth century.

The SRIA followed a quasi-Christian doctrine, which was coupled with beliefs in alchemy, clairvoyance, reincarnation and occultism though it was frequently criticized for an unhealthy preoccupation with materialism. It required initiation and grades of subsequent advancement toward degrees of seniority.

In the twentieth century an active branch of the fraternity was formed in Christchurch, Hampshire, centred on the Rosicrucian Theatre, which was opened in 1938. Among its founder members was Dorothy Clutterbuck, an affluent local widow who had lived much of her life in the East as the wife of a British government official in India, and it was she who introduced Gerald Gardner, soon to found the Wiccan style of witchcraft, to Rosicrucianism. It has been widely believed that the Rosicrucian Theatre provide a "front" for the Southern Coven of British Witches, who were at the time carrying out their activities in Hampshire and were technically outside the law in terms of the 1735 Witchcraft Act.

The SRIA was claimed by some to have provided much of the inspiration for the foundation of the occult Hermetic Order of the Golden Dawn, many of whose rituals aped those of the Rosicrucians. The present headquarters of the Rosicrucian Society are in California, where it preaches a doctrine of reason and promises success to its members.

Opposite: Pilgrims under escort of Knights Templar in sight of Jerusalem, fourteenth century.

QUAKERS AND MORMONS

In the twenty-first century a number of breakaway and innovative sects parade as Christian but owe little to Christian orthodoxy.

THE QUAKERS

The oldest of the three breakaway Christian sects to have achieved prominence during the last 300 years and still be actively in existence is the Quakers. Founded in about 1650 among a group headed by George Fox, an itinerant apprentice shoemaker, they are properly known as the Religious Society of Friends. They gained their nickname because of the notion that, while holding their meetings, they quaked with fear in the presence of God. They constitute the successors to breakaway sects including the Anabaptists. Quakers are largely silent in their style of worship and believe that the Holy Spirit resides within the human soul, which may be guided by this inner light. They also reject many Orthodox Christian rituals, including the taking of the sacrament. During the Cromwellian era they resisted many of the social norms of the Puritans, and refused to recognize the authority of ministers of the Church as well as magistrates. This made them unpopular and identified them in some quarters as potentially dangerous. The impression that they were "oddballs" was not lessened by the fact that many of them practised *glossolalia* – speaking in tongues – a practice still continued among some groups.

Today they espouse largely ecumenical views concerning other Christian bodies and in the past have been active in social reforms. William Penn, an early leader, emigrated to America and founded the State of Pennsylvania, which was originally populated by Quakers. They also spearheaded much of the anti-slavery reforms of the eighteenth century.

THE MORMONS

More correctly known as The Church of Jesus Christ of Latter-Day Saints, the Mormons were founded in New York, at Fayette, in 1830 by Joseph F. Smith as an evangelical missionary sect. Born in Vermont in 1805, Smith first received his religious calling at the age of 15 while working as a farmhand. In 1827, he claimed to have received visionary inspiration from the ancient prophet, Mormon, who represented the early indigenous tribe to whom Christ is said to have appeared shortly after the Ascension. These peoples were descended from three of the lost tribes of Israel. Smith was instructed to write down the text of the Book of Mormon, the original of which was alleged to have been inscribed on gold plates and buried by Mormon's son, Moroni, on a hill at Palmyra in New York State. This book was intended either to replace the Bible or to be accepted as a bona fide part of Christian scripture.

It was Smith's belief that Jesus Christ had been revealed to early immigrants to the New World. They were told that they were to prepare the ground for a new Jerusalem and that Christ was to come and rule their world for 1,000 years. In other words, he promoted a form of millenarianism that related exclusively to the United States of America. On this basis, Smith founded the Mormon Church with just six members, and published the Book of Mormon with the help of a financial backer from among his converts. Like the Quakers, he also espoused the practice of *glossolalia*, and instructed his followers to do so through a highly organized ritual during. He is said to have practised polygamy and enjoyed as many as 80 wives. This startling innovation was justified by claims that Jesus Christ had been married not once, but three times – to Mary of Bethany, Mary of Magdala and Martha – and that most of the Biblical ancients had also practised polygamy.

In 1838, Smith built the first largely Mormon town in Illinois, on the banks of the Mississippi, and its population was swelled by immigrants from overseas, particularly from England. In 1844, however, discontent erupted among the inhabitants of Nauvoo – as the town was named – not least over the polygamy controversy and Smith was arrested.

Opposite: Wagon train of Mormon pioneers on the Oregon Trail, 1879.

With his brother, Hyrum, he was jailed in the county headquarters of Carthage on a charge of treason, but a mob stormed the jail and shot and killed both him and his brother. At the time of his assassination, the population of Nauvoo numbered some 20,000 and the Mormons had spread far beyond the shores of North America.

Smith was succeeded by Brigham Young, who was also from Vermont. It was he who had been sent to England with 12 other disciples to carry out a recruitment drive in the cities of Preston and Liverpool. On his return he was appointed as head of the Mormon Church. Young met with continuing hostility in the American east and decided to make a prudent withdrawal. In 1847, he led 148 of the faithful westward along the Oregon Trail to the valley of the Great Salt Lake in Utah, then owned by Mexico. He founded Salt Lake City on its shores and set about colonizing the area with Mormons. He also instigated various non-Christian practices, and continued to support polygamy.

Brigham Young died in 1877, at the age of 76. Despite a Congressional Law passed in 1862 against multiple marriage, and various subsequent pieces of legislation that resulted in Mormons being imprisoned for their persistence with polygamy, the practice was not formally repudiated by the Mormon leadership until 1890 under its then President, Wilford Woodruff.

Since that time, the Mormons have undergone further reorganization. On the death of Brigham Young they adopted the son of the founder, also called Joseph Smith, as their leader and rejected most of Young's non-Christian doctrinal innovations – though their practices and rituals bear strong similarities to certain of those adopted by freemasonry. They have never lost sight of the interest in multiple marriage and persist in the belief that their souls are destined to speed away to some distant planet from whence they first came. In this far-flung corner of the galaxy they imagine a life as gods, where they may practise polygamy to their hearts' content.

Members contribute 10 per cent of their earnings to the Church. Attempts to leave the Mormon Church necessitate excommunication and frequently result in abuse and intimidation.

The Mormon Church is currently estimated to receive about $6 billion from its global membership and to boost this by another $5 million from its assorted business enterprises; its total assets are said to exceed $30 billion. At the start of 2003, it operated 114 temples worldwide,

with another 14 under construction; it runs 18 radio stations in the US alone and its missionary training centre at Provo in Utah accepts up to 500 new trainees a week for intensive induction courses.

The modern-day leader of the Mormon Church, who has been largely responsible for trying to alter the image of the Church away from that of a cult and toward mainstream Christianity with all the obvious benefits, political and economic, that this entails, is Gordon B. Hinckley. From

2001 onward, under his leadership, there was a move to rebrand Mormonism as "The Church of Jesus Christ".

Cult stigma is, however, hard to shed, and Mormonism continues to include occult and secretive ritual. Those who opt to leave the Mormon Church frequently allege harassment. One ex-member, who has written to the exit website run by former Mormons under the pseudonym Ralph, claims that his family were subjected to emotional blackmail after he left the Church.

"Since they couldn't get to me they turned on my parents. Another example of a repressive, closed-minded church that will work tirelessly to stop anyone who dares express an opinion of Mormonism that hasn't been through the Church's sanitation machine."

Above: Illustration showing handcart-pulling pioneers battling through a blizzard while crossing the Rocky Mountains.

DOOM IS NIGH!

Rooted in the beliefs of many Christian sects is a conviction that Jesus Christ will return to earth in what has been described as "the Second Coming". This they predict will herald the Judgement Day, upon which some form of dreadful apocalypse will unfold and the dead will rise again.

THE PLYMOUTH BRETHREN

Founded in Dublin in about 1827 by Henry Groves and the Revd John Nelson Darby, the Plymouth Brethren represents a loose but exclusive fundamentalist Protestant sect that gained its name after a meeting was held in Plymouth in 1831 to celebrate their first foothold in England. They appoint no clergy, recognize no ecclesiastical order, publish no creed and do not worship in churches. Nor are they particularly evangelical. A schism occurred in 1848, and the brethren divided into open and closed fraternities, with the latter refusing all religious association outside their own restricted membership.

Never a large organization, today the Plymouth Brethren have spread to North America, where they claim some 65,000 devotees in eight distinct groups. In the British Isles, they are now largely restricted to isolated cells surviving among fishing communities in north-east Scotland. Their religion is simplistic and bleak, based on prayer and readings of the Bible. In common with Jehovah's Witnesses, they interpret the Bible literally and believe in an impending Day of Judgement on which they will constitute part of an elite body of humanity who are destined to be saved.

SEVENTH-DAY ADVENTISTS

This group is one of several Christian religious sects that have an implicit belief in the second coming of Christ. This belief is based on various utterances in the New Testament – particularly in the Book of Revelation – and some of the writings of the later Old Testament prophets, including Daniel. There is a similarity between their apocalyptic beliefs to those of both the Plymouth Brethren and Jehovah's Witnesses; they also share views with Christadelphians and the Four Square Gospel Alliance. Essentially, theirs is a philosophy of

Above: John Nelson Darby (1800–1882)

millenarianism, the notion that Christ will return to the Earth to rule over humanity for 1,000 years. Various dates have been predicted for his return but, thus far, none have proved to be correct.

Representing the youngest of a trio of radical Christian sects, the Jehovah's Witnesses have not only always known that Judgement Day is at hand, but have claimed privileged information about when it will happen. They believe that Armageddon will qualify them to rule a new universe with Christ, while the remainder of humanity disappears into oblivion. The Witnesses were founded in 1872 in Pittsburgh, USA, by Charles Taze Russell. His successor, Joseph Franklin "Judge" Rutherford, was no less forthright in his views on the future. These included the belief that a precise number of the chosen flock, 144,000 members known as The Anointed, would travel the expressway to heaven, while the remaining five million members would populate an earthly paradise. In the minds of Jehovah's Witnesses, who subscribe to the ancient pulpit rhetoric of Arius, the Holy Trinity does not exist, but rather the term "One God" means what it says. They also believe that Christ is merely the mortal image of the Supreme Being.

The Witnesses have relied constantly, in their 100 or so years of existence, on predictions of the date of Judgement Day – usually not too far distant – as the most persuasive tool with which to recruit members. The Witnesses take a literal interpretation of the Bible and have thus assumed that the all-important moments of salvation or catastrophe will be presaged by a time of great tribulation. The first date of Armageddon was announced to be 1914, but when that year passed and World War I subsequently came to an end, with the Earth still more or less intact, it was concluded that Jesus had merely paid an unofficial visit in anticipation of Doomsday. Following this anticlimax, first 1925, and then 1975, were set as future options.

Witnesses possess an absolute belief in their exclusive destiny to the extent that Rutherford had deeds drawn up holding his property in trust for Noah, and other Old Testament elders, who would make use of it in the New World. Many members have sold their homes and valuables before the promised dates. The views of the sect are also extreme in other respects. Members refuse military service, stimulants and blood transfusions; they have no clergy but are aggressively evangelical, claiming that other churches are in the hands of Satan and therefore doomed. They also publish *The Watchtower*, a regular periodical disseminating their views.

November 1995 marked a significant policy shift. The leaders of the Witnesses announced that, due to earlier miscalculations, they were no longer able to predict the date of Armageddon, but re-affirmed that the final outcome was not in doubt.

EXCLUSIVE BRETHREN

The Exclusive Brethren are an extremist offshoot group of Plymouth Brethren. However, members of this particular branch of the radical Christian sect believe in taking isolation to even further degrees of severity than the Plymouth Brethren. There are many strict rules and regulations that members must adhere to. Exclusive Brethren are allowed absolutely no contact with the media – they cannot watch television or listen to the radio. They do not allow their children to participate in many social and sporting activities at school. Members of the group also have a strict dress code. There are currently thought to be about 42,000 members worldwide. In 2002, when Don Hales took over the leadership, numbers in the UK were put at 15,000. Since that time some of the more restrictive rules of membership have been relaxed.

Although in the past members of the sect have distanced themselves from worldly affairs, since 2004 there has been mounting evidence of their political involvement in some countries. In 2004, they were linked to advertisements campaigning for the re-election of Australian Prime Minister, John Howard, and in 2006 they used advertisements to attack the Green Party in the Tasmanian state election. Further assaults against Liberal and Green policies were being mounted in New Zealand, where Exclusive Brethren lobbied MPs and paid out some NZ$1.2 million for the printing and distribution of hostile pamphlets. The New Zealand Prime Minister, Helen Clark, went so far as to allege that the group had been involved in spreading "baseless rumour, slander and lies" after it was suggested that her husband, Peter Davis, might be a homosexual.

In Canada, in 2005, it was alleged that the Exclusive Brethren were responsible for an anonymous campaign of intimidation against gay marriage, using direct mail aimed at Senators and identifying themselves as "Concerned Canadian Parents". Similar anti-Liberal and pro-religious right-wing campaigns have been mounted by the cult in recent years in the USA and Sweden.

CHRISTIAN SCIENTISTS

This sect was founded in the United States as the Church of Christ, Scientist by Mary Baker Eddy in the late nineteenth century and was one of a plethora of new and often eccentric sects.

Born in 1821, into a New Hampshire family that believed strongly in the idea of pre-destiny and fate, Mary Baker Eddy developed a deep interest in spiritualism and hypnosis. She came under the influence of a mind-healer, Phineas P. Quimby, who was said to have cured her of an alternately hysterical and depressive mental state. He taught her a homespun philosophy that disease was only the outcome of one's own thoughts and that evil did not exist. Health, he argued, was the natural state of mankind and any deviation from health was of the body's own making.

From Quimby's theories, Mrs Eddy developed her own philosophy, which rejected the objective world and the doctrine of the Trinity. She also became entrenched in the belief that, since God is spiritual and good, reality exists only through the spiritual persona, while other aspects of matter and mankind are unreal and illusory. She believed that illness was the result of malicious animal magnetism and, with this in mind, espoused the principle of spiritual healing. She claimed that forgiveness of sin makes one free from its illusion and that the role of Jesus Christ was to convey this vital message. She was, in a sense, subscribing to the principles of gnosis while seeking to restore what she saw as the original faith and directives of Christianity, which had been eroded down the centuries.

> *"We acknowledge God's forgiveness of sin in the destruction of sin and the spiritual understanding that casts out evil as unreal. But the belief in sin is punished so long as the belief lasts."*

Article 3 of the official summary of Christian Science belief

THE FIRST CHURCH OF CHRIST, SCIENTIST

In 1875, Mary Baker Eddy published her doctrinal work, *Science and Health with a Key to the Scriptures*. Although many of the early copies were destroyed, it became extremely popular reading matter, earning Mrs Eddy substantial receipts. She invested these shrewdly and in doing so provided ammunition for her detractors, who claimed that she was more interested in money than God. The proceeds of her investments, coupled with donations from acolytes, enabled her to establish a metaphysical college in Boston. In 1879 this evolved into The First Church of Christ, Scientist, the original headquarters of which were constructed in the city in 1895. Within the sect she established a hierarchy, accepting no dissent or deviation from the truth as she saw it and refusing

to allow any free-form preaching. Wherever Christian Science existed in the world, its services had to be conducted to a prescribed order with fixed readings from her book, although independent testimony meetings do take place. The Bible took second place and was viewed largely as apocryphal. Holy Communion was rejected since God had not, according to Mary Baker Eddy, been made flesh. Adherents were not permitted to partake of stimulants, including alcohol and tobacco, and among the most ascetic even tea and coffee were forbidden fruit. Mrs Eddy subscribed passionately to the maxim that "God intends men to be healthy and happy", following the Unitarian Universalist so-called theory of optimism.

Despite its rigidly puritanical stance, the sect spread from America to England and other English-speaking societies. Its views, as well as coverage of national and international events, are disseminated through a daily broadsheet, the *Christian Science Monitor*, which was founded in Boston in 1908. The movement does not include an ordained priesthood but its adherents are regarded as spiritual healers and some are authorized public practitioners. On the strength of Mary Baker Eddy's doctrine, Christian Scientists continue to follow an austere lifestyle. They also reject any form of medical treatment, including blood transfusion, since they assert that God will provide salvation from sickness, disease and all other forms of evil. It is this that has from time to time brought Christian Scientists to the fore in the press, when hospital patients in critical states of health have refused conventional medical therapy.

The sect does not enjoy the widespread approval of the Orthodox Christian establishment, which sees in its doctrine a message directed primarily at the more affluent sections of society but with little comfort for the poor, oppressed or hungry. They also point out that if evil is truly an illusion, and God is wholly good, it is illogical that it should constitute any part of conscious existence.

> *"God is all in all;*
> *God is good, God is mind;*
> *God's spirit being all,*
> *nothing is matter."*

Mary Baker Eddy

Opposite: Mary Baker Eddy (1821–1910).

THE MODERN CHRISTIAN ROAD

A number of zealously Catholic fraternities sprang up during the early decades of the twentieth century. They were ostensibly devoted to the worship of Mary, Mother of God, but were, in fact, more interested in stemming the tide of National Socialism in Germany and the burgeoning threat of Communism coming out of revolutionary Russia.

Since as early as the seventeenth century, the national security of many Catholic countries, most notably Spain and Poland, had been placed – as a buffer against Protestantism and Freemasonry – in the capable and at times militant hands of Maria Virgine. But, from about the time of the Spanish Civil War, there developed a flurry of quasi-militant and secretive Marianist clubs, all of them politically right-wing and all claiming Mary as founder and patroness.

OPUS DEI

The most influential and formidable of the fraternities was Opus Dei (Work of God), an ascetic organization founded in 1928 by a Vincentian priest, Fr. Josemaria Escriva de Balaguer, as a counter-measure to what was being seen in Catholic circles as the heretical principles of Freemasonry. Under the patronage of Maria Virgine, it was developed as a splinter group from the powerful Spanish Jesuit Asociación Católica Nacional de Propagandistas, claiming to foster devotion to Mary and teach the Christian significance of work. It was elitist and secretive but in the period following the Spanish Civil War its popularity and strength grew at a remarkable pace. In 1943, it inaugurated a highly occult inner order, the Sacerdotal Society of the Holy Cross, into whose membership – by discreet invitation – came high-ranking politicians and clergy, including bishops and cardinals. Until 1930, when a women's lodge was established, Opus Dei had been an exclusively male club and was strongly backed by General Franco. He placed numbers of its members in key administrative positions so that, by 1958, there existed, de facto, an Opus Dei government in Spain.

Predictably, Opus Dei also came to exert great influence in Latin America. It ran TV and radio stations in Argentina during the 1960s and 1970s and had many of its members in government positions. It was also behind the military junta of 1971. Its message bore a familiar ring – national purification and war against subversion.

On 6 October 2002, the late Pope John Paul II fuelled further controversy when he canonized Josemaria Escrivar, calling him "the saint of ordinary life". This measure did not meet with the approval of critics, including the historian Eamon Duffy of the University of Cambridge, who complained that it was "the most striking example in modern times of the successful promotion of a cause by a pressure group". Other detractors, such as the religion editor at *Newsweek*, Kenneth Woodward, described Escrivar's canonisation as "lightning fast and marred by irregularities". The predictable riposte from the Roman Catholic Church was headed by an Augustinian priest, Rafael Perez, who claimed that the process had moved quickly due to the "promoters' efficiency, reforms in the canonisation process and the importance of Escrivar's figure in the Church".

Criticism of Opus Dei has also come from former members who have used the Internet to set up websites including the Opus Dei Awareness Network, based in the USA, Opus Livre, in São Paulo, Brazil, and Opus Libros in Madrid, Spain, to promote their claims that the organization has hallmarks of a cult. They allege aggressive recruitment of members who are then persuaded not to tell their families or maintain contact with them, are forbidden phone calls and threatened with condemnation.

Concerns have existed for some time about indoctrination. In 1981, Cardinal Basil Hume directed Opus Dei in England to comply with criteria restricting them from allowing minors to make unqualified

Opposite: Pope Benedict XVI blesses the statue of Sant Josemaria Escriva, St Peter's Basilica, 2005.

commitment to the organization, and requiring minors to discuss enrolment with their parents or guardians before making any commitment. He also demanded that anyone should be entitled to enter or leave Opus Dei without undue pressure. However, the Opus Dei Awareness Network has used its website to post personal testimonies, which it claims reveal that Opus Dei has repeatedly violated these guidelines while making false statements to church officials. Some of the authors of the testimonies have opted for anonymity, partly out of fear of repercussions from Opus Dei, but they are said to be verifiable accounts written by sincere individuals who contacted the Opus Dei Awareness Network with the intention that their stories should be broadcast.

The three separate groups have now joined forces as The International Collaboration for Truth about Opus Dei (ICTOD). Their collaboration is described as a coming together of people from all over the world who have had harmful experiences with Opus Dei in places where it operates, in order to challenge statements made by Opus Dei in a recent media campaign aimed at countering the negative image depicted in the best-selling book and subsequent film, *The Da Vinci Code*.

Opus Dei is reported to have focused on the extremes portrayed in *The Da Vinci Code,* including bloody use of the "discipline", or whip, and the "cilice", or spiked chain, while avoiding comment on how the organization takes away personal freedom through a subtle indoctrination process consisting of aggressive recruiting techniques, the withholding of information necessary to make an informed choice and the application of a mix of pressure, fear and guilt to exact blind obedience upon its members. ICTOD intends to focus its resources on making the public more aware of the absolute control and obedience that exists in Opus Dei, along with deceptive and manipulative recruiting practices.

Vatican journalist, John Allen, has claimed in his book, *Opus Dei,* that the organization controls its members through a network of "internal confessors" and a "suffocating degree of structure", which includes interference in one another's conduct by what are euphemistically described as "fraternal corrections". Numeraries, the special higher echelon members of Opus Dei, live in celibate communities, do not go to the cinema or sporting events and are expected to refer to an Opus Dei "database" before reading certain books.

Today it is estimated that Opus Dei includes about 900,000 members. In the UK, one of its more prominent adherents is MP Ruth Kelly – a fact that has caused alarm in scientific circles, where there is concern that Kelly's conservative views may be detrimental to the furtherance of vital stem cell research. An organization representative, Jack Valero, has confirmed that she regularly attends meetings and other Opus Dei events, but in an interview with the *Daily Mirror*, Kelly insisted that her faith is a private matter that has nothing to do with her job. With responsibility for a £1 billion research budget, concerns have been raised that her beliefs may have influenced her judgement.

In 2006, the Italian magazine, *Studi Cattolici*, published a satirical cartoon of the prophet Mohammed depicted as one of the victims of Dante's *Inferno*, which raised considerable anger among Muslim groups. An Opus Dei spokesman was quick to point out that *Studi Cattolici* is not one of their official publications and that the edition had not been vetted, however it is reported that the magazine is "close" to Opus Dei.

THE BLUE ARMY OF MARY

Correctly known as the Blue Army of Our Lady of Fatima, the Blue Amy of Mary was founded in 1947 by the Revd Harold V. Colgan in Plainfield, New Jersey, USA. The tag "Blue Army" was cleverly thought up since it reflected as much a desire to stem the communist "Red Menace", seen by some to be knocking on America's back door by way of Cuba, as the wish to honour Mary's famous blue sash. Its charter was based strictly on the messages of Our Lady of Fatima – whose visions came to the young Dorothean noviciate, Lucia, between 1925 and 1928 in a Portuguese village north of Lisbon – accompanied by warnings of impending free-world conquest, holocaust and general annihilation if the Russians were not converted promptly to Catholicism. By 1950, the Blue Army claimed one million members. By 1953, its ranks had swollen ten-fold and it even claimed converts from active communism. In 1951, Douglas Hyde, then news editor of the *British Daily Worker*, a left-wing journal, openly declared his devotion to Our Lady.

A more public cult than Opus Dei, its members were encouraged to wear a blue ribbon and in later years a Blue Army badge was designed, though its style varied from place to place. In the USA it took the form of a blue medal, in Britain a blue heart, in Spain a blue star and in France a blue cross.

THE KNIGHTS OF COLUMBUS

According to the May 1957 edition of *Life* magazine, the Knights of Columbus represented, "...the world's largest and strongest Catholic fraternal organization solidly based on low-cost life insurance." It also stood equally solidly against the Communist Reds-under-the-beds menace that had been plaguing the USA's imaginative patriots in the post-war years. With their ranks swollen by the fervour of the McCarthyite Communist witch-hunts, they broadcast "safeguards for America" talks on over 200 local radio stations, published a monthly periodical, *Columbia*, which advertised everything from Latex-clad Madonna dolls to Blessed Virgin Nite-Lites, and sponsored major advertising campaigns, backing McCarthy with slogans such as "Our Lady Means Business". In Rome, their most celebrated representative was Cardinal Spellman, who also served as the US military vicar during the Korean War. The Knights of Columbus worked through degrees of initiation and after the third grade were permitted to wear a Columban medal with a star and compasses set around the fasces and crossed with a sword and anchor. In Ireland, the Knights of St Columbanus developed as an offshoot of the Knights of Columbus and was, effectively, a counter-masonic movement. Founded in 1909, they claimed to confront "Orange ascendancy and British socialism" and followed strict codes of secrecy while pursuing the appointment of Catholics to key positions in the city.

THE KNIGHTS OF ST COLUMBIA

One of the British groups stemming from the American-based movement, the Knights of St Columbia, was inaugurated in September 1954 in the altogether more improbable setting of leafy Leamington Spa. In the same year they marched in procession with RAF personnel and others around Wembley Stadium before a crowd of 90,000 Catholics, roaring no less than 3,750 Hail Marys in honour of the coronation of Our Lady of Willesden. Only a few years earlier, in 1948, the Knights of St Columbanus in Ireland had joined forces with the coalition government. They subsequently aligned with Rotarians, Freemasons and Lions International in the promotion of "patriotism and national morality".

In the late 1940s and early 1950s, most of these "Marian armies" had forged links with other groups around the world and presented a formidable body of opinion and anti-Communist activity, particularly since they had, in the main, chosen to abandon their historical antipathy toward such organizations as the Freemasons.

Above: The seal of the Knights of Columbus.

WICCA AND MODERN DRUIDS

The Old English term for a witch – Wicca – was adopted to identify the modern cult of witchcraft when interest was renewed during the early part of the twentieth century.

Although there is a lot of argument about whether today's craft is a survival or revival, there is general agreement that the main branch, Wicca, was created by Gerald Gardner in the late 1940s as a syncretization of beliefs drawn from ancient religious practices. These include those of the Celts, into which has been added various elements of Freemasonry and Rosicrucianism, as well as Egyptian and Classical mythologies and a considerable degree of imaginative invention.

The stimulus for bringing witchcraft out of the closet and opening its doors to a wider membership was the passing of the Fraudulent Mediums Act of 1951. This act gave freedom to an individual to practise so long as their activities harmed no one. A basic tenet of the craft, "...and it harm none, do what thou wilt", was coined in response. Although the various Witchcraft Acts, which had been introduced with steadily more draconian powers since 1542, were repealed in 1736, the position was left somewhat ambiguous since it allowed for the prosecution of persons who allegedly possessed magical powers while also denying the existence of those powers. The 1951 Act resolved many of these uncertainties.

Although the distinctions have largely been blurred, there exists four branches of Wicca that now claim members from around the world – Gardnerian, Alexandrian, Traditional and Hereditary.

Wicca is essentially a mystery cult requiring initiation and a subsequent path of personal fulfilment along with the development of psychic and magical abilities. Advancement requires the passage through various grades or degrees. Its creed is based on a reverence for

Right: A traditional Druid ceremony to celebrate the Summer Solstice at Stonehenge, 1958.

the natural world and the worship of a god and goddess as principles that exist in all of nature, rather than as actual beings floating around in some ethereal realm. The craft is organized in covens of 13 and is open to both sexes – apart from the radically feminist Dianic covens, which are largely restricted to the USA. It is primarily a lunar orientated cult in which eight seasonal festivals, or Sabbats, are celebrated corresponding to the old Celtic festivals of Imbolc, Beltane, Lughnasad and Samhain – the great Sabbats, and with the equinoxes and solstices – the lesser Sabbats.

At the head of the coven is a high priestess, who may or may not be coupled with a high priest, and at the onset of the rites the power of the god or goddess is called down so that it temporarily invades the physical frame of the priestess or priest. Coven meetings are either arranged at open-air venues or in people's homes and involve the inscribing of a magical circle within which a cone of power is raised through mutual psychic energies, drumming and dancing clockwise around the perimeter of the circle. Ritual tools or weapons are employed, including a sacred knife and chalice, and much emphasis is placed on psychic training and exploring personal spiritual abilities in "pathworking".

Although witchcraft can still be worked for maleficent purposes, most is conducted for the benefit of others. None bears any association with Satanism or devil worship since the craft expressly distances itself from the Christian religion of which the Devil is a peculiar invention.

Recent years have witnessed something of a reaction against Wicca, stemming from conservative Christian groups in the USA. In 1999, led by the Georgian Republican representative, Bob Barr, some of these groups campaigned against Wiccan gatherings on US military bases by urging American citizens to boycott enlistment in the army until it terminated what were described as "on-base freedoms of religion, speech and assembly for Wiccan soldiers".

The campaign apparently found little public sympathy and was largely ineffective, especially since President George W. Bush stated: "I don't think witchcraft is a religion. I would hope the military officials would take a second look at the decision they made."

In the UK, tolerance of the Wicca movement has moved a step further and the first Wiccan wedding to be legally recognized in the UK was performed in 2004 under the eye of the Registrars of Scotland.

THE DRUIDS

Druidry stands as the collective name for a group of cultic organizations, many of which are devoted to the pagan traditions of the ancient Celts. Apart from attention to Celtic mythology, Druids place emphasis on poetic inspiration and divination through the use of an arcane alphabet known as Ogam. While some of the Druid organizations, including the Ancient Order of Druids and a number of other friendly societies, operate on a purely charitable status, others pursue more esoteric interests.

The Ancient Druid Order, founded in 1717 by John Tolland, attracted members, predominantly men, whose interests lay in hermetic magic, theosophy and the notion of a God whose existence relied solely on natural reason. Although largely male, the modern Druid priesthood includes the Lady – the Spirit of the Earth – and Druids eschew sexual discrimination. Today's Druids reject the idea of a revealed deity – the idea on which Christianity is based – and accept that everything in the material world emanates from the Sun, a spiritual source from which energies descend as shafts of light. It is to the Sun, they believe, that the spirit finally returns at the moment of death.

The ritual season is based on worship of the Sun and includes, at its height, the Summer Solstice rite, which has been held, traditionally, at Stonehenge in Wiltshire – although the monument bears no known association with the Celtic civilization, but is rather a creation of the earlier Bronze Age. The tradition was championed by George Watson McGregor Reid, a chief Druid who was elected in 1908 and who campaigned actively for the right to worship at the stones. At midnight, on the eve of the Solstice, a silent vigil takes place on an adjacent mound and it is followed by the famous celebration as the Sun rises on the longest day. There are also festivals coinciding with the spring and autumn equinoxes and a more private, reflective rite that takes place at the Winter Solstice.

During the latter parts of the eighteenth and the nineteenth centuries, a number of Druid orders sprang up with similar objectives, many of which still exist and include the Druid Order, The British Order of the Universal Bond, and the Order of Bards, Ovates and Druids, the latter being particularly interested in Celtic mythology and the so-called Earth Mysteries.

Opposite: Pagan celebrations have ancient roots but are still practised today. Druids at Stonehenge, 2014.

THE HORSEMAN'S WORD

Some of the most extraordinary quasi-religious sects have been based on very ancient traditions of secret communication and control over animals.

Horse worship was linked chiefly to the worship of the mother goddess, though there are male Irish Celtic mythological names, including Ro-Ech, which means "Great Horse" and Eochaid.

The Romano Celtic goddess, Epona, was the apotheosis of the horse and she is depicted thus on many altars from the Roman period in Gaul. We also know, from the twelfth-century commentator, Geraldus Cambrensis, of a bizarre horse cult performed by the tribes of Ulster, in which at his inauguration, the chief of the clan bathed in a soup of horse flesh:

The mare being immediately killed and cut in pieces and boiled, a bath is prepared for him [the chieftain] from the broth. Sitting in this he eats the flesh which is brought to him, the people standing around partaking of it also. He is also required to drink of the broth in which he is bathed not drawing it in any vessel, nor even in his hand but lapping it with his mouth.

It is clear that this seemingly grotesque rite symbolized the communion of the goddess and the king who was perceived to be her consort on Earth.

The use of a horse's head in ritual, the origin of the modern hobby horse, which still forms an integral part of cult traditions in towns such as Padstow, Devon, may well go back to prehistoric times. One of the few human figures to have survived from the art of Stone Age Britain, carved on a bone, wears a horse mask.

Because of the horse's vital importance to ancient societies, anyone seen to develop an esoteric relationship with, or exert influence over it acquired a position of respect and often power. Thus, the so-called "horse whisperers" came to enjoy a singular social accord in country districts of the British Isles.

There is a suggestion that the activities of societies of horsemen may extend back as far as Roman times, but the achievements of individual horse whisperers were not generally recorded before the seventeenth century. A county record exists in Sussex, for example, dating from 1648 and noting that one John Young had the art of controlling horses by means of whispers. The cults were active until late in the nineteenth century in the horse breeding areas of East Anglia, particularly around Stowmarket and Newmarket. The secret headquarters of the cult in England was believed to exist somewhere in or near Ipswich. In the remoter parts of Scotland and Ireland, the cults probably persisted until much later, and there is some suggestion that occasional horse whisperers preserve the art even today. In Scotland they were collectively known as the Horsemen Societies and, although operating in great secrecy, they attracted considerable popularity and respect in the eras prior to the industrial revolution.

One of the most celebrated of all horse whisperers was James Sullivan of Cork, Ireland, who was born toward the end of the eighteenth century. He practised his art in strict privacy, like most of his kind, but achieved fame in 1804 by subduing and taming an unusually vicious stallion named King Pippin at Curragh. This animal had resisted all reasonable attempts to bring it under control yet Sullivan managed the feat without recourse to any apparent forcible means.

The ability to horse whisper is said to have run in families and resulted in much rivalry among individuals who claimed to be able to compel the horses under their influence to perform, merely through the use of soft noises, ever more complicated feats of manoeuvre. Inevitably, the art was believed to involve semi-magical skills, but it is known to have relied partly on the use of a vocabulary of words and sounds accompanied by a degree of ritual. Initiation into the cult was open to farm workers and other countrymen who had shown a degree of empathy and ability to work with horses. Once within the fraternity, they were obliged to take oaths of secrecy and were given passwords and trained in the more esoteric aspects of horse whispering.

One of the curious names given to these individuals was Toadmen, since among the devices that the whisperer was rumoured to keep in his pocket was the V-shaped sacral bone of a toad. It has never been revealed how this instrument was used, but it was considered to be highly effective in application. A hugely popular novel was published exploring the theme of the horse whisperer in 1995; this was made into a film directed by Robert Redford in 1998.

Opposite: An 1876 illustration of James Sullivan, the Irish horse whisperer of Dunhallow, County Cork.

THE CHILDREN OF GOD, OR THE FAMILY

On 24 November 1995, a British High Court judge issued a damning indictment of a cult that was founded in California, in 1968, and which, in its day, claimed communes of devotees in places as far-flung as South America, Europe and Australia.

The Children of God began as an innocent gathering of drop-outs among the hippie population of California. They had been attracted to a club, proclaimed as Teens for Christ, by its founder. He was one-time Methodist preacher, David Berg.

Berg followed a well-worn preaching trail by forecasting a doomsday scenario to which America was committed through its imperialist policies and obsession with materialism but which could be escaped by following the doctrine of Moses David, or "Father" David as he styled himself. He was, in his own words, the "Endtime Prophet" who was ready to offer a route to salvation through his "Law of Love". Such a route would, it was inevitably claimed, cost money. This money was destined to keep Berg and his family in affluent comfort while the flock lived in varying degrees of poverty in religious communes. Members of the cult were, at first, taught the desirability of celibacy, but when Berg's burgeoning sexual appetite spilled over to involve the wives of sect members, the message was altered to one of virtually unrestrained promiscuity. This included, it has been claimed, lesbianism, homosexuality, incest and paedophilia. Almost no form of sexual deviance was frowned upon, and pornography was openly circulated, since it was classed as the "Love of God".

Berg also established "Hookers for Jesus". These were attractive women, both married and single, who were commanded to go "Flirty Fishing", or "FFing", around clubs, bars and any other venues where they could find men who were willing to be lured first to bed and from there into the fold.

The name Children of God was not of Berg's invention. It was coined by a journalist and Berg was quick to appreciate its potential, although in 1978 he felt obliged to change it to the more respectable Family of Love.

By the time Flirty Fishing was in full spate, Berg was living in England and addressing his followers through a constant stream of letters. These were broadcast to the acolytes and were sold to the public at large by way of regular pamphlets and broadsheets. The money was funnelled back into the organization and into an increasingly luxurious lifestyle for Berg, whom his devotees came to regard as someone akin to a latter-day Messiah or a Moses.

During the Flirty Fishing era, dozens of women gave birth to children whose fathers were infrequently identified. The cult was supposed to look after these victims of religious promiscuity but rarely carried out fostering duties in any proper manner. Cult members who tried to escape did so with the warning of eternal damnation ringing in their ears and faced the prospect of life in poverty for themselves and their illegitimate dependants, while the outside world viewed them with wariness and distaste.

Toward the end of the 1970s, police in various countries around the world became alerted to claims that the cult's activities included child abuse. By the early 1990s, members had received strict instructions that the internal workings and membership of the Family of Love should be kept secret from the outside world. Police inquiries continued, however, and it was established that in the south of England alone as many as 1,000 children had been recruited over a 10-year period, during which at least 116 had died from a variety of causes.

Prosecutions began in September 1994 and compensation to a victim of abuse was ordered by the Criminal Injuries Board. The sect, however, continued to fight the claim. In November 1995, Lord Justice

---

Opposite: A convert grinning as he is about to be submerged in the English Channel.

Ward declared in the High Court that Berg was sexually depraved and had sacrificed the rights of children on a false altar of misconceived service to the Lord. He found against the cult and permitted a 28-year-old London member to keep her three-year-old son if she agreed to denounce the teachings of Berg. After the hearing, the cult claimed the verdict as a victory.

It is alleged that after the death of David Berg in 1994, the movement was taken over by his widow, Maria, and that he has regularly communicated with her from the spirit world. His messages have been publicized through the cult's newsletter, and claims are made that instructions also come from such celebrities as Marilyn Monroe and Elvis Presley.

Rebranding themselves as The Family, the organization allegedly forecast the end of the world in 2006 or 2007. Presumably with this in mind, its international headquarters is believed to have relocated from Zurich to India toward the end of the 1990s, while its British-based leaders, Gideon and Rachel Scott, left Britain in 1998, heading for South Africa, where the main part of the membership may also have moved. The general opinion among doomsday cults is that the southern hemisphere is likely to be less badly affected than the north in the event of Armageddon. The Family's *Endtime News* pages on the Internet have now dropped a recent forecast of the end of the world in 2006 or 2007 in favour of something imminent but less specific.

In a recent conference on cults, Andri Soti of the London School of Economics claimed that the number of new members of The Family in the UK is extremely small or non-existent, although Gideon Scott argued that this is because recent converts tend to have relocated to foreign fields. Most family members, however, are thought to be second and third generation descendants of the original Berg disciples.

In 2005, the international organization was active in providing relief to survivors of the Asian tsunami, providing donations of milk powder and rice as well as toys, school bags and raincoats for children. In 2006, it also facilitated relief trips to the earthquake-affected regions of Yogyakarta and central Java. A team of 16 members operated for a week in the Bantul area, where teenager followers of the cult helped with the clean-up and participated in programmes and activities for children alongside other local student volunteers in the area.

Today the website of The Family is keen to press home the message that the end of the world is nigh, with a regular feature trendily titled "Endtime News": this labels everything from the flu bug to global warming as evidence that the apocalypse will shortly be upon us. The organization has commercial links with a company called Aurora Productions AG, committed so its promotional pitch runs, to the production and

distribution of educational and inspirational printed, audio and visual products for adults, teenagers, and children. This includes *Kiddie Viddie* announced as "a highly acclaimed series of behaviour-enhancing videos capturing the attention of children from 6 months to 6 years and featuring 54 kid-vid songs fully visualized in a fast-paced, info-packed way!" Other products include a DVD heralded no less enticingly as "provoking an audio-visual experience you will not want to miss!" but entitled *Countdown to Armageddon,* in which you can "discover what earthshaking events are soon to take place, so you can plan your future".

Above: Members of Children of God singing before sitting down to lunch, Los Angeles, 1971.

THE PEOPLE'S TEMPLE

On 21 November 1978, the world woke to news reports of a massacre deep in the jungles of the small South American Republic of Guyana. This was not a political slaughter, nor an illustration of ethnic cleansing, but the bizarre killing of an estimated 917 members of a religious sect.

At first it was believed that all, including 383 American citizens, had been involved in a mass suicide pact, but pathology reports later revealed that as few as 200 died voluntarily – the rest were executed by gunshot. When investigators examined the scene they recovered a total of 39 firearms, including shotguns, rifles and pistols, plus a cache of money in US and Guyanese currency totalling $2.5 million They also discovered a large tub containing the remnants of a lethal cocktail consisting of a powdered children's orange drink labelled "Kool Aid", to which had been added potassium cyanide and tranquillizer drugs.

The bodies lay piled on top of one another, many dressed in their Sunday best, with most of them near the altar in the meeting house. Among them was the body of the cult leader, James Thurman Jones, with his wife and a small child. Reports gathered after the event indicated that many had been forced to drink poison at gunpoint. Those who had resisted or tried to flee into the jungle had been shot by security guards, who then turned their weapons on themselves.

JONESTOWN

The chronicle of events leading up to the horrific climax in November 1978 began in August of that year, when the self-styled Reverend Jim Jones led 1,200 members of his faithful flock to the Marxist paradise of Guyana to start a new life and to prepare for Armageddon. Jones had founded the People's Temple in California, attracting mainly poor people from ethnic minorities with promises of a world in which all would live as equals in Christ. In reality, Jones was never a true Christian believer but

Right: After the 1978 massacre, the hundreds of bodies were strewn all over the Jonestown complex in Guyana.

rather an impassioned follower of Marxism who believed that Christian fundamentalism could be applied to bring large numbers of people under his influence as political converts. He had started churches in San Francisco and Los Angeles and had courted the attention of politicians to gain support for his aims of helping the poor and underprivileged. A charismatic and forceful personality, he duped many influential figures, including then Vice President Walter Mondale, who once entertained Jones aboard his private jet.

At the height of its popularity, the People's Temple was undoubtedly a success, claiming congregations of several thousand worshippers, although some press reports that membership exceeded 20,000 are probably greatly exaggerated. In reality, the Temple may have enjoyed on average about 3,500 devotees. Jones relied on heavy-handed techniques and intimidation to maintain order and loyalty among his flock. Dissent, or the desire to leave the People's Temple, resulted in beatings with wooden paddles, boxing matches in which victims would be

knocked unconscious and exhausting work schedules. Jones also claimed spiritual healing powers. He would draw cancers from the bodies of sufferers and display them in a handkerchief. It was later revealed that chicken guts had been employed to serve the deception. He was also facing charges of financial irregularities and so, with his Californian star beginning to fade, he invested in a 27,000-acre piece of savannah and jungle at Kaituma in Guyana, which he named Jonestown. He also kept an urban headquarters in the capital, Georgetown.

The 1,200 devotees who followed him were housed in huts painted in pastel colours, but the intimidation increased. "Non-positive thinking" resulted in regular kicking, slapping and punching. Inmates were warned the surrounding jungle was a deathtrap of snakes and jaguars. The only practical way in or out of Jonestown was via the rough airstrip.

THE SLAUGHTER

Matters came to a head on 18 November 1978, when US Congressman Leo Ryan visited the commune, accompanied by four pressmen, to investigate reports that American citizens were being forcibly held there. The party attempted to leave but were ambushed and shot to death at the airstrip. The following day, Guyanan troops and other American investigators flew in to discover over 900 corpses. From the few who had escaped came harrowing reports of poison being ladled out by the commune doctor and nurse and announcements via loudspeakers proclaiming the dignity and beauty of death and resurrection. Jones was heard to exhort mothers to shoot poison down the backs of their children's throats. Those who resisted or tried to flee were forced to drink the cyanide cocktail at gunpoint or were mown down in bursts of semi-automatic fire.

When the cult's financial affairs were exposed, it was discovered that the hierarchy had deposited between $10 million and $15 million in banks in Switzerland, Panama and Romania. Jones himself had amassed a personal fortune of more than $5 million.

Right: James "Jimmie" Jones's body is clearly identified by his name scrawled in marker on a US military casket.

THE BRANCH DAVIDIAN

The Branch Davidian was formed as an offshoot of the Seventh-Day Adventists in 1929, when it was known as the Davidian Adventists. Its founder was a Bulgarian-born immigrant to the United States, Victor Houteff, who fell out with the Seventh-Day Adventists after he made a complaint that the half-million membership had become complacent.

His claim was that it needed whittling down to the biblical 144,000 Servants of God. He also claimed that he was the "prophet from the east" who had been chosen to oversee the selection process and to guide the Servants of God to Israel. Once there, they would await the Day of Judgement, to be followed by the new Heaven and Earth. The title of the cult derives first from the assertion in Zechariah 3:8, "Behold I will bring forth my servant, the Branch", and from the Judaic belief that the Kingdom of David would be restored in Syrio-Palestine. Houteff developed the skill of relating biblical narratives to present-day peoples and places, a technique employed by his ultimate successor, David Koresh. He also developed a huge mailing list of more than 100,000.

In the spring of 1935, the cult commune was relocated to a 189-acre piece of real estate not far from the small town of Waco in Texas. Houteff gave it the name of Mount Carmel, perceived it as a staging post prior to the move to Israel, and set about gathering and preparing his 144,000 righteous souls. He died in 1955 and two years later, the Branch, headed by his widow, Florence, sold up and moved to another larger property at Elk, some nine miles east of Waco. Florence Houteff then predicted that the beginning of the end was scheduled to commence in the spring of 1959, the year, coincidentally, of Koresh's birth. When the apocalypse did not descend, many members became disillusioned and left. Florence retired into obscurity and a large part of the holding at Elk was sold off.

THE FINAL MESSENGER

In 1955, however, a new claimant to the role of final messenger and prophet had arrived on the scene. Ben Roden and his wife, Lois, effectively rebuilt the fortunes of the Branch Davidian through the 1960s and 1970s. In 1981, three years after the death of Roden, a disaffected Seventh-Day Adventist named Vernon Howell arrived at Mount Carmel. He became a willing disciple of the elderly Lois, who now headed the commune, and, in the process, developed a sexual relationship with her. He thus engendered a jealous feud between himself and the Rodens' son, George, which was to end in George's incarceration in a mental institution.

When Lois died, in 1986, David Koresh – as Howell came to be known – gained control of the commune and ruled until the disastrous conflagration of April 1993. He introduced ideas of polygamy, group upbringing of commune children, violent resistance to outside authorities and, most significantly, the idea that he was the bearer of the final message of God and the key to the Seventh Seal of the Book of Revelation by which the faithful would be marked and saved from doom.

By 1993, the federal authorities were looking for justification to get inside the heavily armed camp of Mount Carmel after tip-offs that the cult possessed illegal firearms. On 28 February, 76 armed agents of the Federal Bureau of Alcohol, Tobacco and Firearms tried to storm the complex. A gunfight ensued, resulting in the deaths of four BATF agents and six Branch Davidians. A greater number from each side received non-fatal gunshot wounds. The assault was repelled and a stand-off ensued that lasted for 51 days and provided abundant and often lurid media fodder. During that time, the inhabitants of the commune appear to have remained steadfast in the belief that 150 years of Adventist history could not let them down – they truly believed they were God's chosen people.

Opposite: Koresh's mugshot from his 1987 arrest for the attempted murder of George Roden; he was acquitted due to mistrial.

Shortly after sunrise on 19 April, a pair of modified M60 tanks arrived at the perimeter of the commune, smashed through the fences, punched holes into the walls of the buildings and began to pour in CS gas. At first, Koresh remonstrated, but by noon the first smoke and flames were seen inside the main building, which had been torched by cult leaders. Witnessed worldwide by millions of television viewers, the fires and explosions that ensued incinerated 74 cult members, including Koresh, his various wives and children, and his senior lieutenant, Steve Schneider. Nine people escaped to give evidence concerning the days leading up to the carnage, which was generally condemned as a heavy-handed and bungled exercise by the Federal authorities.

Today, the cult clings to existence in the Mount Carmel area but is much-reduced and deeply divided, split into two bitterly opposed factions. One of these is "anti-Koresh" and claims to have been the original movement before Koresh took over. Led by two of the Waco survivors, Clive Doyle and Ron Goins, the group planted a grove of trees to commemorate the victims of the siege and built a small museum on the site of the compound, apparently strongly hostile in tone to both the memory of Koresh and the actions of the US government in 1993. This building, however, was subsequently commandeered by the second faction, including some two dozen members headed by the Pace family. They cut down the trees, one of which had been dedicated by Doyle as "Koresh's tree" and smashed an accompanying plaque claiming that the existence of both amounted to a form of pagan idolatry, rather than a memorial. The Pace group nurtures hopes of recovering ownership of the Waco property at some time in the future.

This remnant of the cult concluded that Koresh would return to earth on 13 December 1996 in some sort of apocalyptic event that would reunite the living with those who had perished in the Waco siege. They relied on interpretation of a somewhat obscure prophecy contained in Daniel 8:14 that speaks of 2,300 days after which "the sanctuary shall be cleansed". When no cleansing actually took place, they recalculated the dates and decided that matters would come to a climax on 6 August 1999. Again, their world did not undergo a shattering transfiguration but undaunted, they continue to meet in the expectation that on a date yet to be determined Koresh will reincarnate and lead them to some new Branch Davidian utopia.

The survivors of Waco hold an annual memorial on 19 April. In 2018, Clive Doyle, one of 9 members who escaped the fire, lead a memorial service to comemmorate the 25th anniversary of the siege. In interviews at the event, Doyle stated that he and other survivors meet weekly, and still believe that Koresh truly spoke the word of God.

Right: The conflagration of the cult compound at Waco, 1993.

THE TEMPLE OF THE SUN

In the early 1980s, a bizarre and ill-fated cult named the Temple du Soleil (Temple of the Sun) was established in Europe and North America. The sect was the inspiration of a Belgian doctor, Luc Jouret, and a failed French property dealer, Joseph Di Mambro.

Together they preached a doomsday message and recruited membership from among affluent or influential families on both sides of the Atlantic, chiefly from Switzerland, Canada and France. Considerable personal assets were given up by cult members and invested in various private properties. Between them Jouret, Di Mambro and his wife, Jocelyn, administered a number of cells totalling more than 500 members, though it has been claimed that, worldwide, the cult attracted as many as 3,000 devotees. Jouret was aged 46 and Di Mambro 70 when they perished as part of a horrific suicide pact. They took with them, ultimately, 69 people, including a number of children.

THE LEADER

Jouret was born in the Belgian Congo and served as a paratrooper in Zaire, where he learned the skills of manufacturing delayed action fire-bombs. He also qualified as a doctor of medicine in Brussels. Jouret became increasingly interested in fringe medicine and in eastern mysticism and, having already visited India to meet with a guru, later joined an unrelated solar cult in France. After a period of time he resigned and set up his own Temple du Soleil, which he claimed was descended from the charter of the medieval Knights Templar. It was his preoccupation with a forthcoming apocalypse, and his belief that he and his followers could be saved by fire, that set him on a course toward emulating the fate of the Knights Templar, most of whom perished after having been indicted as heretics and burned at the stake (see pages 42–3). Jouret took the fundamental principles of Templar faith and modified them for his

own purposes, adding elements of eastern mysticism and debased Roman Catholicism.

Jouret claimed to his followers that he was a time traveller who would lead the faithful to a new life on a planet that was orbiting the star Sirius. He was obsessed with the idea of regeneration through fire and with the significance of 21/22 December, the period of the Winter Solstice when the Sun is at its weakest angle in the Northern Hemisphere. That so many intelligent people, including seemingly well-balanced businessmen, journalists and government officials, were duped into an initiation ceremony of knighthood involving flashing lights, a sword and a chalice, and finally persuaded to end their lives in violence, offers a remarkable insight into Jouret's presence and charisma.

MASS SUICIDE

There are indications that Jouret contemplated a mass suicide in Canada in the spring of 1993, but the plan had to be postponed after he was arrested for flouting Canadian gun laws. Thus, the climactic chain of events that resulted in the deaths of over 70 people did not commence until the end of September 1994, when a husband and wife who had been trying to escape the sect were slaughtered, along with their three-month-old baby, at Morin Heights, near Montreal. Nikki and Antonio Dutoit were stabbed repeatedly and their baby was found with a stake driven through his heart. Antonio Dutoit had been Joseph Di Mambro's gardener and evidence suggests that his family's fate had been sealed by the choice of the name Emmanuel for their son. This had been fiercely opposed by Di Mambro, who had a 12-year-old daughter called Emanuelle. Joseph Di Mambro claimed that his daughter was the product of divine conception, and that Emmanuel Dutoit was the incarnation of the

Right: The smouldering remains of one of the Solar Temple properties, 1994.

Antichrist and had to be destroyed. The killers, Joel Egger and Dominique Bellaton, committed suicide four days later in Switzerland by drugging themselves and detonating a delayed-action petrol bomb. More or less simultaneously, at a cult-owned property at Cheiry in the Swiss mountains, 12 women, 10 men and a child had apparently drunk champagne and then either been shot dead or injected with powerful drugs. Wearing white, red, gold and black cloaks, most of the bodies had been arranged like the radial points of a star, feet pointing toward the centre, to await immolation by a petrol bomb. This failed to detonate and the evidence remained intact.

Further south, at Granges sur Salvan, another 25 corpses were found burned beyond recognition in two adjacent properties owned by cult members. On this occasion, the petrol bombs had exploded. The bodies of Luc Jouret and Joseph Di Mambro were later identified from dental records. The deaths had been broadcast to Swiss and French authorities by a cult member, Patrick Vuarnet, who had mailed the so-called *Last Testament of the Temple du Soleil*, which indicated that the cult

was preparing for a final purification ritual by fire before journeying to a new spiritual life on a planet that was orbiting the star Sirius.

A year later, just two days before Christmas 1995, a macabre sequel was revealed in a forest glade on the remote Vercors Plateau in the French Alps near Grenoble. Sixteen charred bodies, again laid out on the ground in the shape of a star or a magical circle, their feet pointing inward, were discovered after police had been alerted to the possibility of another mass suicide. They had found letters similar to those sent by Patrick Vuarnet the previous year, which contained details of the cult's belief that death did not exist and that a bright light was about to shine on the longest night of the year. It was established that all had perished on the eve of the Winter Solstice, having been drugged, shot, doused in petrol and set alight. The victims included Edith Vuarnet, the wife of a former French ski champion, and their son, Patrick, who had circulated the prophetic warnings. A newspaper report also claimed that two French police officers, Jean-Pierre Lardanchet and Patrick Rostand, members of the cult, had shot the others and set light to them before shooting themselves.

Above Left: Police lay out the bodies of the members found at a Temple farm in Cheiry, Switzerland.

THE
RAJNEESHIS

During the late 1960s, in an emerging climate of free sex, drugs and alternative lifestyles, and where the blight of AIDS had not cast its shadow, a self-styled guru named Bhagwan Shree Rajneesh began to make his name.

His unusual philosophies attracted the attention of many youthful western drop-outs, who made the journey to his spiritual headquarters in Bombay in search of fulfilment. This was convenient for Rajneesh since it provided him with revenue that would have been beyond the means of any of the local population – it suited him to claim that only the rich could find true spirituality. Once under his tutelage, his students were parted from their wallets and, in return, provided with lectures and rose-coloured robes. They were encouraged, on a regular basis, to chant mantras, gain enlightenment, shed the robes, romp nude on the beaches and enjoy sex with as many fellow travellers as was conveniently possible. Thus the cult of the Rajneeshis was born under the auspices of being a centre for religious meditation. It is worth noting that the title Bahgwan translates as "master of the vagina".

Civil indignation at this impropriety forced the cult to uproot and decamp to Poona, lying to the south of Bombay, where it continued to flourish in an *ashram*, or retreat. This consisted of a bungalow that was surrounded by several acres of land and therefore out of sight, and mind, of the local population.

Here, Rajneesh used a compelling mixture of mind-bending meditation and subtle oratory, as well as demands of unswerving devotion, to maintain the total control of his acolytes, or sanyassins. Rajneesh claimed that mysticism was all-important and that the route to unlocking its secrets was through meditation. This meditation could take various forms, including the act of sexual intercourse, although eventually the sex would become unnecessary, for the achievement of enlightenment and celibacy would replace it.

Opposite: Rajneesh and a group of his passionate followers in France, 1979.

SEX, DRUGS AND MIND-NUMBING MEDITATION

The cult became linked with drug running. Its disciples acted as couriers, carrying illicit goods to European cities and returning with cash to swell Rajneesh's funds. Allegations concerning this enterprise were reinforced by a BBC documentary that was filmed undercover. It revealed the extent of amorality among cult members and had such an impact that the cult moved again, this time to the USA. It descended on the small town of Antelope in Oregon, buying a desert property called Big Muddy Ranch. Cult members infiltrated the town council, effectively taking over the civic administration, and renamed the ranch Rajneeshpuram. Buildings were erected at the ranch without planning approval and when local officers attempted to intervene their offices were firebombed.

While all this was taking place, Rajneesh lived a life of considerable opulence that compared starkly with the squalor and dirt in which his commune disciples were obliged to exist. By now, he was keeping order by means of a personal cult police force and through the strict enforcement of a regime that was designed to remove elements of individuality and to increase dependency on the cult. The outside world, including family, past friends and careers, were all considered worthless and meaningless. Rajneesh also enjoyed the sexual favours of a steady stream of young female initiates, whose submission was sometimes little short of rape, and continued to extol the virtues of uninhibited sex. He also ordered regular sessions of mind-numbing meditation, interspersed with frenetic activity, including kicking, screaming, biting and punching, in order to release pent-up emotions.

Eventually a federal investigation team was sent into the commune. They discovered laboratories containing

various chemical and biological agents as well as surveillance equipment and in 1985 Rajneesh was forced the leave the USA. At this time, he spanned the world with almost 600 meditation centres although they are now greatly reduced in number. Rajneesh died in 1990, allegedly as a result of either poisoning or from full-blown AIDS. The Rajneeshis returned to Poona, where their notoriety continues.

In the 1990s, the Rajneeshis changed their name to Osho and now operate through some 20 meditation centres.

THE CULT TODAY

The cult is now run by a Canadian real estate investor, Michael William O'Byrne, better known to his followers as Swami Prem Jayesh. It is said to collect a revenue of up to $45 million a year by "de-stressing" western executives. In 1995, two British women were sentenced by a United States court to five years' imprisonment for plotting to kill a lawyer who was investigating the headquarters of the cult in Oregon. An accountant from Devon called Sally-Anne Croft, whose cult name was Ma Prem Savita, and an aromatherapist from Hertfordshire called Susan Hagan, whose cult name was Ma Anand Su, had funded the purchase of handguns and organized a hit squad to attack attorney Charles Turner in an attempt to prevent closure of the ranch. The women fled to England but were extradited, tried and convicted at Portland, Oregon; they each served a five-year sentence.

Right: Singing and celebrating at a large Rajneeshi gathering in the 70s, Munich, Germany.

JAPAN'S DARK FORCES

Japan has become a nation of cults. At least 180,000 cults are registered, from tiny organizations with a few hundred members to the largest, Soka Gakkai, which is claimed to have members in 8.27 million households, with a further 1.7 million members in 190 countries outside Japan.

At least 17,000 proclaim extreme religious views, yet it was one of the smallest, the Aum Shinri Kyo cult, that attracted global notoriety on 20 March 1995 when its members orchestrated a horrific gas attack on the subway in Tokyo.

Unlike many other sects, whose aim is to escape Doomsday by adopting a radical personal and essentially exclusive lifestyle, Aum was committed, through its leader, Shoko Asahara, to world domination.

Their aim was to change the pattern of materialism for all humankind and thus to escape ultimate godly retribution, due to take place, according to the leader's divine predictions, in 1997. There was good reason to believe that then 41-year-old Shoko Asahara was mentally unstable, but he had been, nonetheless, able to command the total obedience of his followers. The cult was responsible for the release of Sarin-type nerve gas on the crowded Tokyo subway system. This resulted in the deaths of 12 commuters and the hospitalization of several thousand more.

In English, the name of the Aum cult translates as "Supreme Truth". Estimates of membership have varied widely, but the figure of 10,000 during its heyday has dwindled considerably and may now be as little as 1,000. Shoko Asahara was a rather improbable-looking leader. He was squat, short-sighted, had a dark beard and long hippie-style hair, and wore a white jumpsuit and training shoes. To his followers, however, he was The Master, a reincarnation of Imhotep, the builder of the great step-pyramid complex at Sakkara in Egypt, who lived during the twenty-seventh century BC. Imhotep was respected as a sage and an accomplished scribe and, after his death, he achieved a virtually mythical status as the son of the creator god, Ptah, with cult centres both at Sakkara and Memphis, where he was revered as the "Great Physician". His cult continued into Roman times but why Asahara should have taken Imhotep as an idol is unclear.

Prior to launching the Aum sect, Shoko Asahara had followed a chequered though unprepossessing career. Working first as an acupuncturist, he went on to found the short-lived Heavenly Blessing Association. When this collapsed in 1982, Asahara, having been convicted of selling quack health remedies, founded the equally obscure Aum Divine Wizard Association. This also collapsed. The Aum Shinri Kyo cult was launched in 1988, and demanded of its members, mostly young people, that they hand over most of their worldly possessions in order to escape divine retribution. In return, they were subjected to crude forms of brainwashing that required them to wear electrically wired head-gear that delivered low-voltage shocks from batteries strapped around their waists. They were also subjected to sensory deprivation and drugging, as well as near-starvation diets. The chemical factory run by the cult was capable of manufacturing enough Sarin to kill the world's population several times over.

In 1996, one of Ashara's followers, Eriko Lida, was among the first members of the Aum cult to earn a criminal sentence when she was jailed for six and a half years for her complicity in the death of a public notary, Kiyoshi Kariya. In the same year, another member, Ikuo

---

Opposite: A member of the Aum cult dances to commemorate the murder of Hideo Murai, one of the highest-ranked members, 1995.

Hayashi, received a life sentence for his part in the Tokyo subway gas attack. Since that time, 11 Aum members have received the death sentence. In January 1997, the Japanese government failed in an attempt to have the group disbanded and, in the summer of that year, it expanded to 27 centres in Japan. In January 2000, the cult changed its name to Aleph, and Rika Matsumoto, the third daughter of Shoko Asahara, took charge. In February 2004, Shoko Ashara was finally found guilty and sentenced to death; the Japanese Supreme Court rejected his final appeal in September 2006.

SOKA GAKKAI

The Soka Gakkai sect has maintained a lower profile than the Aum Shinri Kyo cult, but is thought by many observers to pose a greater long-term threat to Japanese society. Soka Gakkai came into existence in 1930 as the lay branch of a Buddhist sect, Nichiren Shoshu, and is now Japan's largest religious cult. It began to gain notice in the press in the early 1960s, shortly after electing a new leader. Daisaku was determined to take the sect to a position of power by recruiting members on a large scale. He subsequently adopted autocratic control, commissioned icons that bore a striking resemblance to himself, instructed his acolytes in the benefits of renouncing worldly things and demanded, predictably, large donations from them. Allegedly, only some of the wealth that was amassed by the sect has been passed on to cultural and charitable organizations and to the peace movements it claims to support.

Meanwhile, the cult has enjoyed immunity from any tax or criminal investigation under Japanese law, which protects any and all religious corporations from scrutiny. The sect is accused of carrying out a covert long-term campaign to infiltrate the government and assume political control. Since 1998, the political wing of the cult, the Clean Government Party, has been known as the New Komeito Party. In the 2003 and 2004 elections, it did well, thanks to the substantial voting power of Soka Gakkai. In the summer of 2005, New Komeito proposed to form a coalition government with the Democratic Party of Japan if the DPJ gained a majority in the House of Representatives. In August 2005, that opportunity failed to arise when the general election resulted in the Liberal Democratic Party winning a substantial majority. New Komeito, however, then struck a deal with the LDP and is currently enjoying a majority coalition.

THE PATRIOTS

21 February 1996 began as a normal day at the Caswell Shooting Range in Mesa, Arizona, with the usual mix of the security conscious and the gun-happy taking up positions on the firing range and blasting away at targets.

The pace of events continued uninterrupted until two of the clients, a young British pair on a motoring tour of the USA, turned away from the range, placed their guns in each other's mouths, nodded a mute countdown and shot themselves to death. A few hours later, and 1,000 miles away near Redding in California, a third Briton attached a hosepipe to the exhaust of her rented car, closed the windows and, as the vehicle filled with carbon monoxide fumes, shot herself in the head.

THE MILITIA

Within a few days, an unconfirmed rumour began to spread that Stephen Bateman, Ruth Fleming and Jane Greenhow, all British university graduates, had travelled to America to join the extremist right-wing sect, Militia. The three had ended their lives dressed in military-style uniforms, but what added to the speculation surrounding their deaths was a note scrawled on a doctor's appointment card and discovered in the hotel room used by Bateman and Fleming. Apart from a neo-Nazi rank, Obergruppen-fuhrer Stattspolizei, it included the words "eternal agony hell".

One of the most recent, but also the most sinister, millennium cults, the Militia is among the hardest to find. It possesses no sectarian headquarters and one cannot find it listed in any telephone directory. In May 1995, one of its coterie reduced the Federal Building in Oklahoma City to rubble. The excuse for this atrocity was difficult to determine because Militia logic is based on the slightly eccentric notion that the US government, the gun control lobby, chemical warfare, genetic mutations, UFOs and certain secret military bases throughout North America are all part of a grand conspiracy to dispense with United States sovereignty and to turn the world into a kind of Orwellian nightmare super-state. The Oklahoma bomb was detonated on the second anniversary of the

Waco massacre in which David Koresh and most of his Branch Davidian sect were self-immolated at the end of a siege by Federal agents. Their action was mounted on the suspicion that the Waco compound was holding illegal arms. It has been claimed that what took place in Oklahoma City was some kind of retribution against the Federal authority.

THE PANIC PROJECT

In response to the perceived threat to the American way of life, a plethora of quasi-military organizations has sprung up, known loosely as the Militia or the Unorganized Militia. Their spokesperson seems, currently, to be an Indianapolis attorney, Linda Thompson, who works from the offices of her American Justice Federation. These groups, in effect local uniformed gun clubs, support no central hierarchy but are linked by common aims and fears, by the technology of the Internet, and by a scattering of short-wave broadcast stations, among which Radio Free World, run by Anthony J. Hilder, is not untypical. A Beverly Hills resident and lesser-known Hollywood movie-maker, he believes that Hollywood is part of a government conspiracy to dupe the population with subliminal propaganda of the kind which he claims is evident in such films as *Close Encounters of the Third Kind*. Most of the radio stations reflect the extreme right wing of political opinion and claim that the US government is waging war against the principles of freedom. They point to secret military bases, such as that codenamed Area 51 in the Nevada Desert. Officially, it does not exist, but detractors believe that a new generation of super weapons

is being developed there. They claim that these weapons are explained away as UFOs and that a scenario is being rehearsed there, and at other similar establishments, for a fake alien invasion of Earth. To combat this imagined threat – the so-called Panic Project – the militias exhort the use of violence. "Shoot the sons of bitches!" is a familiar sentiment which seems to have been taken to heart when the Oklahoma bomb was planted by Timothy McVeigh, who was subsequently convicted and executed by lethal injection in Terra Haute Federal Prison, Indiana, on 11 June 2001. One of the focuses of resentment is a select caucus of influential people, known as the Illuminati. It is claimed they are a splinter group from within the upper echelon of the Society of Freemasons.

"I present to you that the peaceful citizens of this nation are fully justified in taking whatever steps may be necessary, including violence, to identify, counter attack and destroy the enemy ... You must prepare to fight and if necessary die to preserve your God-given right to freedom."

William Cooper

Opposite: Emergency services descend on the aftermath of the bombing at Alfred Murrah Federal Building in Oklahoma City.

BLASTING SATAN

Gun control is a particular area of antagonism for the militias, since they see the aims behind it directed as being conspiratorially toward the "soft underbelly" of society in the USA leading, ultimately, to the genocide of the American people. They demand the right to hold arsenals in order to protect their future and believe that the next President of the USA will be "one of theirs". Among the front runners for this post was the leader of a militia group at St. Johns, Arizona, named William Cooper. An ex-navy serviceman, he published a journal called *Veritas*, and wrote a handbook on the predicted American dissolution called, appropriately, *Behold a Pale Horse*. In these publications, he offered a mixture of God-given and

gun-given homespun righteousness and doomsday warning that is anti-Catholic, anti-Semitic and anti-press, and which warned of a new order – with Pope John Paul II and George Bush high in its rankings – threatening the millennium. He claimed that with the dawn of the year 2000, the secret chambers of the Pyramid of Giza would be opened, its secrets revealed and Satan would ride out – with only the American militia blasting away to stop him. From the spring of 1999, Cooper lived as a virtual recluse with two dogs and some chickens for company. He died in a shoot-out with law enforcement officers in Apache County, Arizona, in November 2001, after threatening passers-by with a handgun.

THE NINE O'CLOCK SERVICE

The more overt aspects of the Sheffield-based modern evangelistic phenomenon that was known as the Nine O'Clock Service were bathed in limelight for several years. Few, however, were aware of the more covert activities of its leader, Christopher Brain.

The Nine O'Clock Service represented a Christian revolution and was seen by many churchmen as the way forward, a magnet to draw youth back into churches. Christianity broadcast through compelling words, music and images projected onto giant screens. It possessed all the electronic attraction of a rave gathering.

What has never been in doubt is that Christopher Brain was highly successful in drawing people – especially among teenagers and younger age groups – who had become disenchanted with the more traditional forms of worship into the fold of his Nine O'Clock Service. So successful was the experiment that the Nine O'Clock Service was able to take over a large conference and leisure centre in Sheffield in which to conduct its worship.

Above: The Reverend Chris Brain lectures at the large Nine O'Clock Service centre.

ORIGIN OF THE SERVICE

The Nine O'Clock Service first became established at St Thomas's, an Anglican church with an evangelical tradition and a vicar, Robert Warren, who was from the outset sympathetic to the ideals promoted by Christopher Brain and his immediate circle. Brain was eager to dispense a political message. He was against the middle-class style of church-going behaviour, professing himself in favour of a simple lifestyle, a communal purse and "doing not thinking". In 1985, after a visit from an American evangelist called John Winber – who went on to found the Toronto Blessing – Warren was persuaded that his church needed an influx of young people and that Brain should be allowed to start his own Christian rock gathering. The most convenient time for this gathering was nine o'clock on a Sunday evening, after the more conventional service. It would be a style of worship based on the club culture.

The Nine O'Clock Service began with about 50 people and very rapidly grew to between 200 to 300, and ultimately, as many as 600 members. Devotees were urged to hand over money, possessions and considerable amounts of time. The service was held in a darkened church, with images projected onto walls and screens and pop music playing before the service started. The service was described as exciting and fun. It immediately attracted large numbers of young people who would not otherwise have attended church services and was enthusiastically supported by the Bishop of Sheffield, David Lunn. In 1990, the Bishop of Sheffield officiated over one of the largest confirmation services ever experienced in the Diocese, with more than 100 candidates.

During the months that followed, Brain not only cultivated close friendships with a number of young women within the congregation but also began to enjoy inappropriate relations with them. Furthermore, he was steering the Nine O'Clock Service further and further away from its original purpose and meaning. Senior Church representatives would visit Sheffield and leave claiming that Brain was a latter-day prophet. He used this approval to enforce an increasingly autocratic style of leadership.

EARLY WARNING

In 1992, the first person to speak out publicly against Brain and the leadership did so by going to the Bishop of Sheffield with her doubts and concerns about what she perceived as injustices within the organization. Her pleas fell on deaf ears. The Bishop was, she claims, fairly dismissive and once her dissent became known within the Nine O'Clock Service she was ostracized and forced to leave. For its part, the Nine O'Clock Service media machine rubbished her claims and put forward a familiar cult refutation, the suggestion that she was mentally ill.

Notwithstanding this early rumble of disquiet, so successful had the Nine O'Clock Service become that it outgrew St Thomas's and was relocated to a large modern conference hall in the centre of Sheffield. The Archdeacon of Sheffield became increasingly involved with its activities, and in so doing put a public stamp on its respectability. The thrust of the Nine O'Clock Service message had, by this juncture, moved away from fundamentalism and toward a more environmental and ecological theology and Brain had instigated a different focus of service, which became known as The Planetary Mass.

THE CONGREGATION SPEAKS OUT

In August 1995, and in Brain's temporary absence, disenchanted members of the congregation found the courage to make public their concerns. The full story of the personal corruption and abuse going on behind the scenes of the Nine O'Clock Service was exposed, first in the press and then in a frank television programme in the *Everyman* series. During the programme, several women who had been sexually compromised spoke of their disillusionment with Brain and of the damage that had been done to their lives. As one worshipper, Sara, said afterwards on BBC's *Everyman* of the Nine O'Clock Service: "He regularly would talk about how we were discovering a post-modern definition of sexuality in the Church. Again, it's language covering up what was really going on – one bloke getting his rocks off with about 40 women."

The Church of England braced itself to be censured in the "sex for Jesus" scandal of the decade. The Church was accused, forcefully, of failing in its duty to protect parishioners. The Nine O'Clock Service proved to be an acute embarrassment to the Anglican Church, who having first applauded and abetted their aims, were obliged to concede to having made an utterly flawed assessment.

SCIENTOLOGISTS

The Church of Scientology claims currently to enjoythe devotion of seven million members worldwide, which puts it among the largest, wealthiest and most influential of all religious sects.

As its science-fiction-writing founder, Lafayette Ronald Hubbard, posited at an authors' convention in 1950, four years before setting up the Church of Scientology, "Writing for a penny a word is ridiculous; if a man really wants to make a million dollars he should start his own religion."

INTER-GALACTIC ENTITIES

Although Hubbard had no recognized religious training, he established the Church of Scientology in 1953, off the back of earlier projects, including the Hubbard Dianetics and Research Foundations and his personal assembly of science theories, Scientology. The Church of Scientology preaches a curious mixture of science fiction, physics and religion. Members are taught that their bodies are merely vehicles for inter-galactic entities – said to be billions of years old – called Theta-beings, or Thetans for short. While these beings are extremely powerful, their strength is undermined by influences known as Engrams, which are caused by anything from inter-stellar wars a few millions of years ago to fellow Thetans exercising healthy rivalry. The result of Engram "implantation" is disease and disability, both physical and mental. The way to identify Engrams is with a gadget known as the Hubbard Electro-psychosis Meter, or E-meter, and the way to neutralize their effect is through a combination of psychotherapy and confession, a process referred to as "auditing".

The movement's headquarters were incorporated in the USA in Los Angeles in 1954 as the Church of Scientology of California, having been first incorporated in New Jersey in 1953. Then, in 1959, a manor house with extensive grounds that was to be the future British base for Scientology was purchased at Saint Hill, near East Grinstead in Sussex. Other centres followed, in the form of franchises that paid into the "Mother Church". Eventually, all the main Scientology centres came to be named after the British manor house at Saint Hill.

During the early 1970s, Scientology members infiltrated the US Inland Revenue Service and established that a major IRS investigation of its tax affairs in California was about to commence. Large numbers of IRS documents were stolen in a covert operation and, in 1977, the FBI responded with raids on Scientology offices. In the aftermath, 11 members of the sect were arrested and sentenced to imprisonment. The IRS case was, nonetheless, to continue for an unprecedented 14 years while the Scientologists argued their corner.

In 1981, some five years before Hubbard's death, his heir-apparent, David Miscavige, one of the most trusted Messengers, instigated a purge of members with whom he did not see eye to eye. This resulted in major repercussions from disaffected ex-Scientologists, most notably Jon Atack, who wrote a damning indictment under the title *A Piece of Blue Sky*. This too resulted in a protracted court battle in which the headmistress of one of the Church schools tried to suppress publication of the book. The book was subsequently re-edited. Another detractor has been Larry Wollersheim, a former member, who instigated a suit against the Scientologists in Los Angeles that has been running for a good number of years.

The most controversial judgement in recent years has been that given in favour of the Scientologists in the IRS dispute. It was the longest-running case in IRS history when, in 1993, the American courts decided in favour of the Church of Scientology.

Today, according to authorized Scientology information, *Dianetics* has sold over some 22 million copies, while the famous Hubbard E-meter is currently offered to British customers for only £2,600. The

Opposite: American actor Tom Cruise making a speech at the opening of a new Scientology church in Madrid, Spain.

Above: Large crowd at the inauguration of a Scientology church in Milan, Italy.

headquarters of Scientology remain in Los Angeles. Full-time staff at all Church branches have worn blue outfits in the style of a US navy uniform in honour of Hubbard's contested war record. A few years ago, the organization orchestrated a massive advertising campaign in various world centres, lighting up electronic messages in London, New York, Russia, Tokyo and Mexico which, it claims, were viewed by 30 million people.

Overall control is in the hands of David Miscavige who, like his predecessor, has become increasingly reclusive and is rumoured to be protected by large numbers of trained, gun-carrying bodyguards. Miscavige affects the title Captain or Commodore – as did Hubbard.

Currently, the membership of the Church in the UK alone is thought to number as many as 100,000. Scientology has achieved publicity in recent times through having attracted A-list celebrities to its ranks, such as Tom Cruise, Juliette Lewis and John Travolta. However, it has also received a number of well-publicized setbacks in Europe and the USA. As early as 1997,

Scientology was outlawed in Greece when a court in Athens passed judgement that its "financial machinations were not compatible with public welfare". In November 1999, a French court convicted one of its former officials, Xavier Delamare, on fraud charges and issued a suspended sentence of two years' imprisonment plus a 100,000 Franc fine. In Spain there was a similar turn of events after the Madrid State Attorney's office issued an indictment against 18 members of the sect demanding 30 years' imprisonment on charges ranging from tax evasion to the formation of an illegal organization and the promise of cures with the support of proper education or permits.

In December 1999, the UK Charity Commission barred the Church of Scientology from charitable status on the grounds that it did not promote "the moral and spiritual welfare of the community" nor confer a "public benefit". The Church's brushes with the law have continued. By 2000, the French authorities were recommending the dissolving of the Church of Scientology on the grounds that its activities threatened public order. In June 2001, Olga Ukhova, head of the regional Scientology centre in Khabarovsk, Russia, was jailed for six years on charges of money laundering and it was alleged in court that the centre had been responsible for impairing people morally, materially and physically.

A major setback in the United States occurred in May 2002, when the Los Angeles Superior Court ordered payment of compensation amounting to $8,647,643 to former member, Lawrence Wollersheim, after Scientology counselling practices were found to have "driven him to the brink of insanity". He had then spent 22 years battling for compensation, during which time the Church of Scientology had repeatedly refused to pay and launched successive appeals. It also filed suits against him in an attempt to force him into opting for settlement or dropping his case altogether. In the same month, though in an unconnected case, one of its ministers, Reed Slatkin, pleaded guilty to a $593 million fraud after an investigation by the US Securities and Exchange Commission. According to one assessment in 1999, Scientology had already been involved in some 1,500 out-of-court hearings and had the distinction of being the most litigious of all so-called religious movements.

In 2001, the Council of Europe branded Scientology a cult as distinct from a church or religion and noted its ability to drain individuals of money and self-confidence through manipulation and hard-selling techniques. Supporting evidence for this criticism is not hard to discover. In December 2002, Scientology members posing as health workers reportedly targeted students at University College, Dublin, in a membership drive using anti-drug pamphlets in a bid to open contact with thousands of potential members. The leaflets, delivered to the students' union were all printed with contact numbers for Scientology members and the students' union, was subsequently contacted several times urging them to take more pamphlets. The College said it refused to hand out the information once it realized the religious sect was behind the campaign.

These problems did not, however, deter the Church of Scientology from opening a grandiose multi-million pound new premises in the City of London in October 2006. According to Paul Lewis, a reporter for the *Guardian* newspaper who attended one of its recruitment courses, a 30-minute video for initiates ends with the programme presenter advising that anyone is free to turn their back on Scientology, but they should beware, as "that would be stupid … you can also walk off a bridge or blow your brains out."

In November 2006, BBC News reported that the City of London Police were carrying out inquiries amid claims that officers had received gifts worth thousands of pounds from the Church of Scientology. More than 20 officers were allegedly targeted over a 15-month period.

THE SEA ORG

In 1967, having purchased three sea-going vessels of varying worthiness, Hubbard renewed his wartime acquaintance with the ocean and launched a maritime branch of Scientology named Sea Org, of which he was the self-appointed commodore. The move was largely to escape the growing problems that the cult was facing on land. Hubbard, with his crews, sailed around various parts of the world, putting into harbour for as long as possible at any one time, while remaining unrecognized by local authorities. A team known as Commodore's Messengers waited on his every whim and members of the crew were subjected to rigorous and often brutal conditions aboard ship, where draconian punishments for disloyalty were meted out to adults and children alike.

THE FAMILY FEDERATION FOR WORLD PEACE AND UNIFICATION

Anyone who followed events reported in the media in February 2000 cannot fail to have noted the extraordinary circumstances of a mass satellite- and Internet-linked wedding of around 450,000 couples at the Chamsil Stadium in Seoul. This event moved the marriage brokering efforts of Sung Myung Moon on to a new level.

Formerly colloquially known first as the Moonies, then as the Unification Church, before adopting its present title, The Family Federation for World Peace and Unification, Reverend Moon's organization was founded in Korea in 1954. Moon believed that he had received a message from God directing him to continue the work that Jesus Christ had failed to complete 2,000 years earlier. To this end he wrote his own Bible, entitled *Divine Principle*, which was to guide and inspire his disciples worldwide. IFFWPAU members are forbidden stimulants such as alcohol and cigarettes; sex before marriage is also forbidden. Although the organization gained most of its converts in Japan, there is a sizeable following in America, England and a number of European countries. The group first established a toe-hold in the USA in 1959, and in 1972 Moon decided to move his entire base of operations to New York State. In the late 1980s, they expanded into mainland China and in 1990 persuaded President Gorbachev to permit the recruitment of members in Russia.

MONEY AND POWER

Moon has espoused a vision of global dominance for his religious empire; he has also proved himself adept at raising large sums both through donations from converts and from street selling, making his financial enterprises an open agenda.

In a published article of 20 April 1999, the National Network of Lawyers Against the Spiritual Sales claimed that from about 1975, the Church was able to pocket enormous sums through "spiritual sales strategies", including the marketing of such products as Ginseng extract and marble urns. Many sources allege that between 1975 and 1985 the Unification Church in Japan remitted 5–10 billion-yen monthly to Sun Myung Moon. Even today, believers in Japan remit more than 10 billion yen each year.

There are reported to be more than 50 organizations linked to FFWPAU in Britain, with various innocuous titles. Members evade revealing the ultimate destination of funds received, if necessary by lying to cash donors. A former recruit has claimed that she was able to take as much as £400 a day selling pictures to the unsuspecting public. According to her she was, at one time, the top Unification Church money-maker in Britain. She also claims to have been an expert in "heavenly deception", the art of concealing from her punters exactly whom she was working for. "Telling lies", she is quoted as saying, "isn't a sin in the Moonie religion." Such activities are strongly denied.

The Moon organization enjoys a charitable status that has, at least once, in 1988, come under serious threat. At times it has expended massive funds on advertising and public relations campaigns on television and in the press,

Below: A 1992 mass wedding at the Olympic Stadium in Seoul, South Korea.

as well as in legal fees for various court battles. In 1981, an unsuccessful libel action brought against the *Daily Mail* cost the Unification Church £750,000 – an amount that was thought to be unparalleled at the time.

In 1982, Moon was indicted on charges of tax evasion and the organization put $5 million into a public relations exercise designed to cleanse his image. By 1998, The Reverend Moon was in more trouble. It was being claimed that old associates were suing him for $60 million, and his former daughter-in-law was also writing a book in which she claimed to reveal a saga of drug abuse, sexual abuse, gambling and domestic violence behind the walls of Moon's opulent estate Belvedere in Tarrytown, on the banks of the Hudson River in New York State.

Luxury seems to have become a byword in the Moon household: when one of his 13 children developed a passion for horse riding, the *New York Post* claimed that he promptly had a $10 million equestrian centre built for her in Britain, and invested £25,000 in the rearing of racehorses.

The FFWPAU owns assets across the globe on a vast scale. In Brazil alone these are thought to be worth nearly $250 million. The FFWPAU's Brazilian estate extends to some two million acres and it owns an entire town across the border in Paraguay. The Brazilian regional State Assembly set up a commission to investigate the organization, and according to the *BBC News*, in 2000 an investigation was opened there for alleged money laundering, tax evasion and abetting illegal immigration.

Exploring Reverend Moon's business empire has been likened to embarking on an archaeological dig. One of more than a dozen Moon family companies in the US is an armaments company called Kahr that has been traced through an intricate chain of firms to a holding company, Unification Church International – hardly, it might seem, an appropriate business for an organization espousing world peace to be connected with. Kahr was founded in 1993 by one of Moon's sons, Justin Moon, who, observers believe, will inherit his father's empire. The weapons that the company has manufactured include the K9, a small, easily-concealed pistol firing large caliber bullets. In 1999, Justin went on to purchase Auto-Ordnance, maker of the famous "tommy gun", and he has grown Kahr into one of America's top privately-owned handgun manufacturers, with sales of around $20 million a year.

Perhaps in order to improve his image, Moon chose the year 2000 to announce preparations for a grandiose new FFWPAU headquarters to be sited in the coastal town

of Yeosu South Korea. "Headquarters" is a euphemism because, through a business deal with the Tongil Group, a South Korean industrial conglomerate with numerous subsidiaries in heavy industry and food, Moon envisaged the construction of a large resort occupying some 60 acres, with a focus on tourism and the leisure business. According to reports, the resort is scheduled for completion around 2010 and will include "a global cultural town, golf courses and time-share condominiums".

In 2000, Moon was also busy laying the foundations to extend his political influence in South-east Asia by setting up the so-called Inter-religious and International Federation for World Peace. Through this organization he has handed out a multi-million dollar "development aid package" to the government of the Marshall Islands, with the idea of establishing a Pacific government task force to concentrate on economic and development issues in the region. To encourage the way in which these issues progressed he then pledged $2 million to each participating country. In July 2001, it is suggested, as an added enticement, he handed over a generous gift to the Pacific island of Tonga in the shape of two naval patrol boats.

Above: Over 3,000 couples took part in this mass wedding ceremony at the Cheong Shim Peace World Center, South Korea.

THE EXIT ROAD

Although the post-war cult phenomenon was up and running from the late 1950s, it was not until the news broke of the horrific mass suicide at the Jonestown People's Temple in 1978 that concerned parents and relatives began to look urgently for counselling services aimed at helping those who were trying to free themselves from the grasp of religious sects.

One of the prime objectives of many of the cults was, and still is, to remove all sense of independence from members and to promote a physical and psychological gulf between them and the outside world. Most indulge, in one sense or another, in forms of brain-washing and intimidation. To leave or even to speak out against a cult is not only to face excommunication and what is perceived as the very real prospect of damnation in the eyes of God, but to risk mental or physical abuse. This can take many forms. In the extreme it may result in the assassination of the ex-cult member, but psychological pressure is more commonplace. In one recent and not untypical case, a coffin bearing the name of the person being victimized was paraded past their house. Often years of abuse follow the leaving of a cult. This emanates from other cult members living in the neighbourhood and enormous damage is wrought to individuals and families. It is calculated that well over a million Americans have been, or are, members of cults.

Until the early 1970s, little was known of life inside cults or the effect on the mainly young individuals who joined them. Virtually no resources were available to assist those who wished to return to normal life. Those who did emerge were seen, by those who had been close to them, to be psychologically altered and often appeared to behave as little more than programmed robots.

CULT BUSTERS

The term "cult busting" is a popular phrase that has little meaning. Historically, the families of members were self-taught in the methods of liberation from the hold of a cult. They established the techniques of assisting with reconnection to normal family and secular life and those who had been successfully deprogrammed went on to form a network of cult counsellors. There is, however, no sense of breaking or busting cult structures, nor is there a policy of involuntary deprogramming. In fact, today's cult counsellors frequently prefer to make contact in public places since it is not unknown for them to have to defend law suits over claims that cult members have been beaten or otherwise victimized by counsellors working on behalf of parents. The criticism is sometimes levelled that they use techniques of mind-bending in their counter-indoctrination that are comparable with those of the cults. The counsellors are often themselves the subject of threats and intimidatory tactics.

De-programming – detaining a cult initiate in a non-cult setting – used to be an accepted technique but today it is generally frowned upon unless the circumstances, in terms of physical and psychological danger, are severe. Voluntary-exit counselling has to be adapted carefully, and infinitely, to meet the individual's needs. One of the foremost professionals in the counter-cult battle is Ian Haworth, a former member of a Canadian sect. He claims that he has identified up to 26 different mind-controlling techniques used by the cults. He classes himself as an anti-cult campaigner rather than an exit counsellor.

Often the most effective counsellors to assist in liberation from a specific cult are those who have at some time been cult members of the organization, as they will be familiar with its methods. One of the best-known in the United Kingdom is an ex-sect member and

Christian Evangelist, Graham Baldwin. The strategy used by counsellors like Baldwin must take into account the personality and needs of the individual and the nature and consequences of the particular cult's involvement. The individual's experience at the hand of the cult, and their reasons for wishing to escape or not escape, must also be taken into account. Exit advice can also be obtained from the Cult Information Centre in London.

In some cases, and in a practice from which most exit counsellors distance themselves, the cult member is unaware of the role of the counsellor they meet and may not believe they need rescuing. This opens the way to the argument voiced by detractors of exit work, that individuals who join cults may already possess a tendency toward fanaticism and as former members they may be equally zealous in their opposition.

"It is dangerous because it is out to capture people, especially children and impressionable young people, and indoctrinate and brainwash them so that they become the unquestioning captives and tools of the cult, withdrawn from ordinary thought, living and relationships with others."

Mr Justice Latey, rendering an assessment of Scientology in the High Court

Opposite: New members were coerced into cult through systems of brainwashing and manipulation, leaving them vulnerable.

SATANIC

Throughout the ages, few religious beliefs and practices have captured the imagination to the same degree as Satanism and Black Magic. Satanism is a peculiarly Christian phenomenon that involves a pact with the Devil, and has nothing to do with modern Paganism. It relies on a belief in the existence of the Christian Antichrist, Satan or Lucifer – the fallen angel. Witches, who have been erroneously associated with Satanism, reject the Christian doctrine and dogma and so they are, by reason of their beliefs, incapable of diabolism.

Black Magic relies on the darker aspects of the magic arts and is based on medieval sources known as grimoires or clavicles. Like any other aspect of human endeavour, the occult has been open to abuse and so from there it was but a short step to the Black Sabbat and the arts of diabolism – attempts to communicate with evil spirits for evil purpose.

Both Satanism and Black Magic constitute a very genuine plague on societies worldwide and can be used to appalling effect on the uneducated, the naive and those with unfettered imaginations. In Western society, though, the incidence is extremely limited and, more often than not, is the stuff of sensational news headlines rather than sober reality.

THE FIRST BLACK MAGICIANS

The advent of belief in Black Magic and evil spirits arose long before the first Satanic cults appeared. Before the dawn of life in settled agricultural communities, the peoples of the primitive world were drawn together only in scattered hunting tribes, a very few of which have survived into comparatively modern times in remote regions of the globe such as Siberia.

Most of these clans have held a belief in animism, perhaps the simplest and yet also the most imaginative form of religious belief. Animism recognizes that everything, living or otherwise, is part of a constantly varying chain. It follows that, with the right kind of magic, a man can become a tree, a whale can transform into a rock and a bird can appear as a cloud. All of these confusing changes are at the whim of the spirit world and a spirit can also transform, in an instant, into objects from everyday life such as a running deer, a flame in the hearth or a cooking pot. Thus, primitive tribesmen followed the safe principle that nothing is necessarily as it appears.

The shaman is the tribal priest who can mediate with this complicated world of spirits at a level of expertise and intelligence not shared by ordinary people. Shamans go by many names but their purpose is always to act as the honest broker between the supernatural world and the temporal earth, and this puts them apart from the rest.

A few of the northern hunting tribes, including those living in the Kamchatka Peninsula, which points down toward the Sea of Japan, were investigated as late as the turn of this century, before the machinery of Christianity reached them. In their own logic there is no Heaven and Hell – in the moral sense that a Christian would recognize – and therefore no idea of Satanic character, although there are benevolent and malevolent spirits. The unseen world existing in parallel with their own is, however, figuratively bursting at the seams with spirits, since everything in the natural world possesses a supernatural guardian. Thus, the day-to-day activities of each mortal individual are fraught with risk – make the right move and the relevant spirit will shine on you, make the wrong one and your action may result in misfortune. This notion instilled itself into popular Christian belief and still persists among such sects as the Christian Scientists, to whom illness is divinely brought and may not be interfered with by medical science.

The role of the shaman is exceedingly complex, changing with circumstance and according to local tradition, but the job of the black shaman, the archetypal black witch, is to dispense summary justice for the spirits of the underworld. In the typical Siberian pantheon, the spirit realm exists on three distinct levels, the highest being that of the Creators. Beneath them is an army of ethereal beings – some friendly, some malevolent – who watch over their own specified domains of nature. A third group, or sometimes one horrific individual, lives somewhere beneath the world. They are seen as vagrant beings who are essentially evil but not associated with any natural objects. It was from the idea of these underworld creatures that the Nordic world of darkness, the *Niflheim*, evolved and was later popularized by Richard Wagner in the operatic cycle, the *Ring of the Nieblungs*.

SHAMANISTIC RITE

The black shaman has been greatly feared for the powers at his or her disposal to bring misfortune, to the extent that in many tribal societies each family has employed its own personal insurance in the form of household guardians. Their purpose is to repel the dark influences that may be threatened. If the black shaman considers that the spirits of the underworld have been offended he will dispense rough justice in their service.

Dressed in his full regalia, the Siberian shaman can present a terrifying sight to the susceptible imagination. He carries a large, circular drum consisting of hide stretched tightly over a round wooden frame. This is beaten with a stout stick. His typical dress includes a cloak made of darkened skins adorned with long tassels and strings of coloured wooden beads or bones. The face is largely hidden by a pointed cowl-like cap. This is hung with leather thongs and beads to provide a mask-like curtain that effectively conceals the human identity

behind it. Strange as it may appear, the roles of black and white shaman have been known to merge, with the same individual performing both functions as the need has arisen. The key to the shaman's power, irrespective of the role, is the ecstatic trance, the method by which he or she gains access to the spirit world. Under the influence of hallucinatory drugs, the shaman sees that which the ordinary person cannot see and converses with entities that cannot otherwise be heard.

Unfortunately, very little of authentic shamanistic rite has been recorded. Much of the effect lies in the occult nature of the shaman's art and technique. When demonstrations have been arranged before outside ethnologists, there has been a strong suspicion that they have been contrived as party

Above: A Navajo medicine man in costume representing Zahadolzha, a Navajo god, 1907.

pieces for the benefit of the visitors. From the little that is known it would appear that the black shaman may puff on a ceremonial pipe or ingest narcotics in some other way. Then, under their influence, the shamen will sing, dance, beat on his sacred drum, impersonate the sounds and movements of animals and finally render the appropriate justice on his victim, either directly or from a distance. As with the art of Voodoo, much of this would appear to be a psychological threat to which the victim succumbs by a form of primitive, self-induced, mind-bending.

THE HAMMERS AGAINST HERESY

In the early decades of the thirteenth century, after a period of comparative peace within the Catholic realms, a phenomenon that had been almost forgotten was to raise its head once more in a climate where the ecclesiastical rich grew richer and the already poverty-stricken congregation grew poorer – heresy.

THE PAPAL INQUISITION

In order to combat what the papacy saw as a growing threat to its influence, Pope Gregory IX set up arguably the most infamous commission of inquiry in human history, the Papal Inquisition. Although legal penalties were already being meted out against heretics, the Inquisition was the first official body with a specific mandate. Established in about 1233 in the wake of the crusade against the Cathars in southern France, its role was to seek out heretics in areas where the local populace held a sympathetic attitude toward their unorthodox beliefs. The Inquisition did not have powers to penalize but rather to detect those guilty of heresy, by fair means or foul. It travelled a circuit and its proceedings were conducted in secret. Only the sentences were publicized at High Mass in the cathedrals each Sunday. The general premise, however, was that those hauled before the Inquisition were guilty until proved innocent, and the sole objective of the commission was to obtain a confession. There were no acquittals and a released individual was always liable to be rearrested. Ironically, it was Pope Innocent IV who sanctioned the use of torture by secular authorities to ensure that innocence was rarely established, but since the transfer of authority for this activity to the civil courts proved too impracticable, the inquisitors gave themselves the authority to torture those indicted. Each inquisitor was directly responsible to the Pope and the commission was set up only in areas where heretical activity was known. Thus, the Inquisition never came to the British Isles.

Not only did the commission deal with the more serious cases of overt heresy, it also detected witchcraft and sorcery since, by 1398, these were considered to involve a pact with the Devil and therefore to be indivisible from heresy. Offenders found guilty could have personal possessions seized by the ecclesiastical courts

– to whom they were passed by the commission – and could also be imprisoned or executed. One of the more bizarre powers held by the Inquisition was the power to exhume the remains of a person found guilty of heresy after they had died and burn them. The death penalty, though, was infrequently demanded, even during the pious heat of the heresy trials that characterized much of the first half of the thirteenth century.

The Inquisition enjoyed no central co-ordinating body until 1542, when Pope Paul III reformed the Inquisition and established a Holy Office in Rome to oversee its activities. The Inquisition's role had diminished during the fifteenth century, largely because it had actually conducted its affairs with great effect. If heretics continued to exist, they were by then becoming too circumspect to reveal their beliefs publicly. The Inquisition continued, however, until the eighteenth century, before being abolished first in Italy in 1782, and in Spain in 1784. By 1800, moderate religious intolerance was the norm throughout France.

MALLEUS MALEFICARUM

First published in 1486, the *Malleus Maleficarum*, which literally means the Hammer of Evil Doing, was one of the most influential early printed books and was also of direct relevance to the workings of the Inquisition. The document's authors, the German Inquisitor, Heinrich Institoris. and his Dominican colleague, Jakob Sprenger, were working under the direction of Pope Innocent VIII. Two years earlier, Innocent had put his seal to a papal bull issued in Germany, the *Summis Desiderantes Affectibus*, which represented the culmination of efforts made by the Catholic Church to formulate a style of prosecution for witches. This also had the effect of endorsing the papacy's support for the continuing work of the Inquisition.

Left: Pope Gregory IX
receiving a list of the accused
from a kneeling inquisitor,
fourteenth century.

Institoris and Sprenger listed the essential features of witchcraft as they were perceived by the Church. These were, in essence, the renunciation of Christian principles, and any act performed in the service of diabolism.

More specifically, the *Malleus Maleficarum* identified that most witches were women, accusing them of such acts as sexual pacts with the Devil and claiming that they were involved in the initiation of unbaptised children into the craft. The book also claimed that they possessed the powers of levitation and shape changing, that they regularly defiled the Eucharist and were versed in the preparation of magical ointments and potions.

As a document, the *Malleus Maleficarum* proved so popular that it was published in 14 editions during the next 35 years, although there was no English translation until recent times.

THE SABBATIC GOAT

Since the very beginning of recorded history, spirit beings have been depicted as having human form but with distinctly animal characteristics. In the mythology of Greece and Rome, the more risqué deities, in the form of Dionysus, Bacchus and Pan, were often given goat-like characteristics in company with their entourages of Satyrs.

A beast that was half-goat, half-stag made an appearance in the Dionysian Mysteries.

Caprids, members of the goat family, with their horns and their slitty eyes, have been frequent contenders for the role of the antagonist in the natural world. It is not illogical that they should have become transposed to represent the Antichrist in Christian faith. In the art of ancient Mesopotamia, it is goats that are frequently seen rising in challenge to the Tree of Life, the symbol of the mother goddess and Queen of Heaven. In Nordic descriptions of Valhalla, the fortress of the gods, it is a goat named Heidrun that gnaws destructively on the foliage of the World Ash Tree, Yggdrasill. The fleeting description given of the Great Beast that arose from the earth and therefore from the nether regions of the underworld in the *Book of Revelation* has, however, stimulated most of the imaginative descriptions attributed to the Christian devil, who was variously titled Satan or Lucifer, the bringer of light.

Almost any group accused of Christian heresy was also fair game to be indicted on charges of goat-worship. The twelfth-century Valdensian heretics are seen in the frontispiece to the *Tractus Contra Sectum Valdensium*, by Johannes Tinctoris, on their knees before the exposed rear of a somewhat docile-looking caprid. To understand the implications of this frontispiece, one has to examine the polemical Christian claims arrayed against heretics and witches. Both groups were accused of the unsavoury practice of kissing the Devil's anus during ritual worship.

The Devil is depicted as a rather more anthropomorphic goat in Goya's famous, if rather misinformed painting, *The Sabbat*. This picture was painted in about 1794, when ideas of witches performing devilish deeds still lingered in many people's minds, if not on the British statute books – the last Witchcraft Act was repealed in 1736. A haggish sorority is seen offering a skeletal infant to a goat-like individual who has a distinctly mischievous expression around his hairy features and a wreath of ivy leaves entwined in his horns. Witches were considered to be Devil-worshippers for much of the medieval period and the Sabbat was regarded as the nocturnal gathering during which they worshipped their master and engaged in sexual rites with him. It was also an occasion on which, it was commonly believed, they killed babies and young children for an assortment of heinous purposes. In reality, their crimes probably amounted to little more than stealing milk from a herdsman's cows and seeking shelter in his barn.

The link drawn between witches and the worship of a devilish goat arises, in part, from a confusion over iconography. Witches subscribe to an old Pagan faith that does not include the purely Christian character of the Devil. The deity to whom they offer worship – Cernunnos, the horned god – does, however, bear some physical similarities to the imaginative portrayal of Lucifer. Lucifer's image was largely modelled on the classical depictions of Pan, in that he bears the antlers, hair and hoofs of a stag. It is also true that such deities as Frigg – who was the Queen of the Witches in Nordic religion – are closely associated with goats, along with an assortment of beasts that they use to transport themselves from place to place.

ELIPHAS LEVI AND THE SABBATIC GOAT

By far and away the best-known among comparatively modern depictions of the Sabbatic Goat is that of the French magician Eliphas Levi. Despite his heretical beliefs, Levi actually began his career in the Roman Catholic Church, leaving it in 1836. He made his drawing in 1856 and used it as the frontispiece to his *Dogme et Rituel de la Haute Magie*. Levi's goat is a thoroughly Satanic creature, possessing the arms and torso of an androgynous human being, along with black wings, a reptilian abdomen – complete with the caduceus of the ancient Greek god

Hermes, positioned to resemble an erect phallus and entwined serpents – and the malevolent head and feet of a caprid. A magical pentagram is emblazoned on the forehead. Levi had added the not wholly innovative androgynous aspect and drew heavily on the symbolism of past traditions.

Aleister Crowley (see pages 110–11) one of the most famous of the modern occultists and black magicians and a devoted student of Eliphas Levi's work, styled himself the Great Beast 666 after the creature of the Book of Revelation. Crowley was, perhaps, the personification of the twentieth-century Sabbatic Goat.

Above: The Sabbatic Goat, from *Transcendental Magic: Its Doctrine and Ritual*, Éliphas Lévi, 1856.

BLACK MAGICIANS AND THE BLACK MASS

Black Magic and White Magic are somewhat subjective terms since one person's benefit may be another's misfortune. The same may be said for black and white magicians.

Many a wizard or witch has been praised by a beneficiary while being condemned by his or her neighbour. There have probably only rarely been cases of individuals so evil and depraved as to practise the occult arts solely in pursuit of malevolent or destructive ends.

The rituals of black magic have largely been based on medieval magical texts collected into handbooks known as grimoires. These were frequently based on the apocryphal Hebrew Qabalistic magic described in esoteric works such as the *Testament of Solomon* and the *Books of Enoch*.

MODERN-DAY DEVIL WORSHIP

Evidence of suspected Black Magic rituals occasionally emerges even in recent times. In February 1996, police exhumed the body of a local Rotherham man, Jack Mansfield, who had died of natural causes two months earlier, aged 86. Mansfield had been buried in an unmarked grave in a private woodland but the grave had been desecrated and the corpse decapitated. The severed head had been found lying by a roadside 22 miles away. Police confirmed that they were not ruling out some form of Satanic ritual as a possible motive although it was also possible that the outrage was directed at the directors of the burial ground, against which there had been opposition.

In October 2004, Satanism in Britain again hit the headlines with the case of Chris Cranmer, a technician in the Royal Navy who became the first registered Satanist in the British Armed Forces and was thus allowed to perform satanic rituals aboard ship.

At least four specific handbooks of Black Magic, all written originally in French, have been in circulation and are still widely studied and used by occultists. They include: the *Grimorium Verum*, which is based on the magical writings of Solomon the Hebrew Rabbin, and translated from Hebrew early in the sixteenth century by a Jesuit monk named Plaingière; the *Grand Grimoire*, the provenance of which is unknown but which is alleged to have been edited by one Antonio Venitiana del Rabina, although this was probably not his real name; the eighteenth-century manuscript entitled *True Black Magic or the Secret of Secrets* and ascribed to one Iroe-Grego, who is said to have made the translation from an earlier Hebrew work in Rome in about 1750; and the *Constitution of Pope Honorius the Great*, also published in Rome and dating back to 1670.

The Black Mass, popularized by fiction writers such as the popular novelist Dennis Wheatley, is little more than a parody of the Roman Catholic Mass in which the Eucharistic host, stolen from a church, is desecrated or replaced by material such as a turnip that has been stained black. Other features include the backward recitation of the Lord's Prayer. For a Black Mass to be performed correctly, a defrocked Catholic priest should be in attendance. The presence of such a person would be improbable today, but there is evidence that in earlier times clergy were actively involved in aspects of both witchcraft and diabolism.

The number of cases of illegal black masses brought to trial is comparatively small. In England, in 1538, Mabel Brigge was executed for enacting a Blackfast in an attempt to secure the deaths of Henry VIII and the Duke of Norfolk. In 1645, Matthew Hopkins exposed an alleged witch whose familiar bore the name "Blackfast".

In France, the Black Mass was reported for the first time in the reign of Louis XIV. In 1680, several priests, possibly as many as 50 or 60, were charged in the Chambre Ardente with sexual abuse and the sacrifice of children during so-called Black Masses. Among the more lurid reports was that the ceremony was said to require the priest to perform a largely unspecified rite over the naked body of a girl, spread across an altar. At the climax, he consecrated the host over her belly and inserted a portion into her vagina before performing sexual intercourse with her and finally washing her with holy water from the chalice, which was, allegedly, the urine of a goat sprinkled from a black aspergillum.

The desire among practitioners of witchcraft, and others, to misappropriate the Sacrament became so strong that in 1215 the Lateran Council decreed that the Eucharistic vessels, communion bread, holy oil and water should be locked away to prevent their theft and use for magical purposes.

There is some evidence that the Black Mass is still practised nowadays, amid great secrecy, in various parts of the world, including Britain and the USA.

Opposite: The Sabbat – sixteenth-century engraving based on The Arras Tribunal of 1460.

THE HELLFIRE CLUBS

In 1734, the Dilettanti Society was founded with the intention of combining the cultivation of artistic knowledge with conviviality. It drew its membership from among the ranks of the English intelligentsia and well-to-do.

The Dilettanti Society came about in the reign of George II and in the climate of the Whig Supremacy under the ministry of Robert Walpole. It marked a time when England's influence in Europe was waning and was only a few years before she went to war, alone, against Spain. The society attracted men of taste, such as Lord Palmerston, but also lured less respectable young rakes, characterized largely by hard drinking and wealth. One such man was Sir Francis Dashwood, the fifteenth Baron le Despenser.

Dashwood was born in 1708, and had grown used to a pampered and adventuresome lifestyle. In 1738, he found himself in Florence, where he was initiated into the Freemasons and gained a taste for the occult. The following year, he returned to England and became a member of the Dilettanti Society. He went on to found his own club, the Friars of St Francis of Wycombe, a pretentious title for a secret club in which members dressed as monks or friars. This, however, was the limit of their non-secular activity for they used their meetings to eat and drink to excess, gamble and indulge in sexual romps. They represented one of several such clubs that came and went during the eighteenth and nineteenth centuries and which were the focus of scandalous society gossip. The activities of these Hellfire Clubs – as they came to be known – became the subject of rumour when they were linked with Satanism and Witchcraft. They actually had very little to do with Satanic practices but thoroughly enjoyed the salacious reputation they acquired.

In 1751, Dashwood purchased an extensive property at Marlow in Buckinghamshire known as Medmenham Abbey. He set about converting it into a cult headquarters, equipping it in a pseudo-Gothic style and liberally decorating the grounds with pagan statuary. The grounds included a grotto and it was here that club members, dressed in their monastic garb, enjoyed their hedonistic parties. Among those initiated were many prominent names of the period, including Benjamin Franklin, Francis Duffield, Lord Sandwich, George Selwyn and John Wilkes.

John Wilkes was typical of the men who joined the Hellfire Clubs. The son of a wealthy distiller, he had enjoyed a fashionable education and had risen in the world, purchasing a parliamentary seat in Aylesbury. Despite being cross-eyed, he showed a successful propensity for womanizing. He also showed a leaning toward gamblers and other men of doubtful reputation, which brought him close to financial ruin. By the same token he despised what he saw as lesser men who sought refuge in hypocrisy, concealment and "playing it safe". The Hellfire Clubs offered him precisely the reckless and raunchy excitement that he desired.

For most members, the attraction of these clubs was short-lived. By 1762, Dashwood's Hellfire Club had dwindled in popularity to the point where it was obliged to close through lack of support. In the same year, Dashwood took on the role of Chancellor of the Exchequer, a position that he held with great ineptitude until the following year. His only other significant post was that of Postmaster General, which he held from 1770 until his death, in 1781, at the age of 79.

Although they were symptomatic of a comparatively brief era in English social history, in their time the Hellfire Clubs provided a hushed agenda that was envied in many more respectable London salons. Their role in revivals of belief in demonolatry was wholly artificial – little more than an excuse for lurid sexual licence. European salon society had become too secular to believe in impish creatures with curly tails and toasting forks.

Opposite: Satirical catoon of Sir Francis Dashwood worshipping venus.

ALEISTER CROWLEY – THE GREAT BEAST

Born in 1875 in the town of Leamington Spa, England, Edward Alexander Crowley, who changed his name to Aleister, was, depending upon the perceptions of his critics, either the Devil incarnate or one of the most brilliant exponents of the occult arts of recent times.

Crowley's parents were strict members of the Plymouth Brethren group and were probably instrumental in his acquiring a strong aversion to the Christian faith as a young man. He received the benefits of an education at Malvern College and later at Trinity College, University of Cambridge, where he failed to graduate. By this time he had developed an active interest in the occult and there is an unsubstantiated rumour that, while at Cambridge, he is alleged to have met the notorious Essex cunning man, George Pickingill, who may have initiated Crowley into one of his East Anglian witch covens.

At the age of 25 he joined a magical sect, the Hermetic Order of the Golden Dawn, in which he adopted an occult name, Frater Perdurabo. His initiation caused considerable dissent among other cult members, who saw him as an undesirable newcomer, verging on the insane and showing homosexual tendencies that should have barred him from continuing membership. He persisted with the order, however, at first protected by one of its founders, S. L. McGregor Mathers, with whom he later feuded bitterly. Crowley also found himself under the tutelage of a fellow occultist, Alan Bennett, who provided him with an insight into the Jewish magical texts of the *Qabalah* and who introduced him to the obscure magical discipline of *Abra-Melin*, which derived from Greek satire.

THE BOOK OF THE LAW

In 1903, having moved to a house at Boleskine in Scotland, Crowley married a psychic medium called Rose Kelly, the sister of the artist Sir Gerald Kelly, and the couple travelled extensively, including a significant visit to Cairo, Egypt. It was there, in April 1904, that Crowley allegedly encountered a spirit source named Aiwass and was instructed, through the mediumship

of Rose, during a period of three days, to write perhaps his most influential work, the *Liber AL vel Legis* (the Book of the Law). It was in this three-chapter prose poem that he coined his famous hedonistic catchphrase, "Do what thou wilt shall be the whole of the law. Love is the law, Love under Will". At the same time he proclaimed himself, "The Great Beast 666, Prophet of a New Aeon", a curious title that seems to have been adopted from the imagery of the terrifying biblical creature of Revelation that had fascinated him since childhood. It also highlighted his claim that the current order would dissolve into chaos, that a new aeon would arise and that orthodox religions would be overturned. At least in part, Crowley proved to be an accurate prophet.

ORDO TEMPLI ORIENTIS

In 1912, Crowley was initiated into another cult, more secretive than Golden Dawn, called Ordo Templi Orientis. This cult, founded in 1904 in Germany, claimed to follow the Templar tradition. Crowley achieved the rare distinction of being immediately initiated in the ninth degree and rose to become the first British head before succeeding Theodor Ruess as the cult's international leader. Never a widely recognized cult, the doctrine of Ordo Templi Orientis included a confused mixture of oriental philosophy and European tantrism. It was probably little more than a splinter group of disaffected eighteenth- and nineteenth-century Hermeticists and magicians, but it claimed to possess the key to all masonic and hermetic secrets and it proclaimed a strong emphasis on sexual magic, nature lore and freemasonry. Ritual trappings included a ceremonial garter, and a dagger and chalice that represented a symbolic sexual intercourse. The Ordo Templi Orientis operated nine active grades, above which rested a purely administrative tenth grade. The first six grades were awarded by initiation and the rest gained only through teaching. Its activities in Germany were curtailed by the Nazis in 1937, when all occult organizations were outlawed. At one stage during the inter-war years, Crowley also established the notorious so-called "Abbey of Thelema" at Cefalù in Sicily, where he ran training courses in his New-Aeon cult. This was curtailed when Mussolini expelled Crowley from Italy, amid an assortment of lurid allegations about the practices of the cults, and he returned to England.

ADDICTION

Crowley possessed a rapacious sexual appetite, a weakness for the use of narcotics and a yearning for personal power. He found many of the answers to these needs in Black Magic, toward which he drifted steadily from his university days. He wore a medallion around his neck engraved with the sign of the Great Beast, 666, and branded his lovers with the same mark. There is a celebrated photograph of one Leila Waddell with the mark tattooed between her breasts. He also affected a seven-headed "Demon Stick". Contrary to popular opinion, though, he was never a witch and it is claimed that he had an enduring fear of witchcraft, but he succeeded in corrupting and destroying the lives of an uncomfortable number of people who came under his influence, including his wife, Rose, who deteriorated into a hopeless alcoholic before his premature death.

Toward the end of his life he became addicted to heroin and retired to a private hotel, *Netherwood*, near Hastings, where he died in 1947, at the age of 72. Accompanied by scandal and outrage to the last, he was cremated at Brighton accompanied by readings from his magical pagan works and, on his request, his ashes were sent to his successor as head of Ordo Templi Orientis, Karl Germer, who had emigrated to the USA. He had also stated that the members of the cult were to meet on the first anniversary of his death for a dinner in London. Reportedly, only Germer attended.

Opposite: Crowley posing in the "Sign of Pan", next to a book featuring his occult name "Perdurabo" Magister.

THE WITCHES OF SALEM

In the spring of 1692, in the small New England town of Salem, Massachusetts, some 24 kilometres (15 miles) north-east of Boston, now the suburb of Danvers, two little girls aged nine and eleven indulged in what should have been a harmless game. Unfortunately, this game was to have devastating consequences with echoes that reverberate to the present day.

The children decided to try and establish the identities of their future husbands by means of divination. They were carried away by their own play and their dabblings in magic brought on a degree of hysteria and erratic behaviour. That one was the daughter of the local minister, Samuel Parrish, was to be not insignificant during forthcoming events because when he called on medical assistance the local physician, Dr Griggs, was unable to discern a physical cause and put the symptoms down to witchcraft. Once this ominous information was broadcast in the village, not only did the girls become worse, developing convulsions, but the hysteria started to spread and various other women became influenced by what was almost certainly the power of auto-suggestion.

At this juncture the children were subject to serious questioning by the local authority and, whether as a malicious prank against adults they disliked or for other reasons, they identified two local women as being responsible for their distress. The women named were Sarah Goode, a local down-and-out pipe-smoking eccentric, and Sarah Osborne, a society lady whose name had been tarnished by sexual scandal and who had not attended church in more than a year. They also pointed the finger at a young slave girl, Tituba, and while the older women stoutly denied the accusations, Tituba was ready to confess all in lurid detail, admitting that she had liaised with a "black, hairy, long-nosed devil". The two small girls, perhaps luxuriating in the theatrical limelight, continued with their displays of diabolical possession, regularly descending into screaming fits and convulsions, causing the general public alarm to spread further and further afield. Predictably, an increasing number of people not only exhibited symptoms, but were keen to blame their distress on their neighbours.

HISTORY REPEATS ITSELF

New England had fallen under the spell of witchcraft some 50 years earlier, the first hanging of a witch having taken place in Connecticut in 1647. Its effects were considered a serious problem and in 1689 the influential theologian, Cotton Mather, published a staunch defence of belief in the existence of witchcraft in his *Memorable Providences Relating to Witchcraft and Possessions*. He also tacitly supported the witch trials. Salem was, thus, by no means the only place to conduct witch trials, though it was undoubtedly the most infamous, as a single unproved incident resulted in the deaths of 19 people, mostly women, on the gallows. Ironically, the person who had set the wheels in motion, the young slave girl, Tituba, was not among them. Those who confessed to witchcraft were not executed under the New England laws.

The trials were attended by a good deal of publicity and the small girls at the centre of the controversy put on convincing displays of psychological disturbance during the hearings. Tituba, meanwhile, continued her graphic confessions and ominous mutterings about others, as yet un-named, being equally responsible. The effect was that of a snowball rolling down a hill, with more and more names being dragged in. When they had all been indicted the executions had to await the arrival of a new governor, Sir William Phips, but they commenced on 10 June with a single hanging. A further five were sent to the gallows on 19 June, followed by another six on 5 August. By 22 September, 19 people had died and many more were imprisoned. Among those executed were Sarah Goode and Sarah Osborne.

Although witch hunting was generally the preoccupation of the Catholic Church, it found willing participants in the close-knit agricultural communities of the American Puritans, who had their austere lifestyles and zealous Bible-thumping orthodoxy to guard them against

Left: Title page of Cotton Mather's polemic against witchcraft.

Satan. After the Salem executions, the hysteria spread to neighbouring towns to the extent that it threatened to run out of control. Finally, at the end of 1692, with the local prisons bulging at the seams and the authorities at their wits' ends, Governor Phips decided to reprieve all of those who had been indicted and released them from imprisonment. There is no evidence as to whether any of those convicted at Salem did, in fact, indulge in witchcraft. It seems probable that the young slave girl, Tituba, in common with most of her long-suffering compatriots, was interested in and practised what was to become known as Voodoo as a spiritual link with her ancestral roots. Such heathenism was universally condemned by the slave owners as a demonstration of crude witchcraft and diabolism since it was also seen as a focal point of potential unrest.

The Salem witch trials represented a case of local religious politics gone mad, but also reflected a more widespread atmosphere of intolerance within the American colonies of the seventeenth century. Persecution on religious grounds, though less draconian, was rife, and the principle of lawfulness of dissent was not tolerated generally.

In less than a year, the Salem phenomenon had passed, though the appalling indictment of a society that had become blind to reason was to remain, placing an irrevocable blight on New England's record of justice.

RITUAL KILLERS FROM DEATH VALLEY

In July 1969, the murder of a Californian musician, Gary Hinman, went virtually unnoticed by the media. He had been stabbed repeatedly at his home and the words "Political Piggy" had been scrawled on the wall in blood.

On 9 August 1969, however, the world's press reported the horrific murder of several prominent people in Benedict Canyon, a wealthy residential district of Bel Air, California. It is an area of large private estates favoured by the Hollywood chic. One of the properties had been rented by the film director, Roman Polanski, and it was there that his pregnant 26-year-old actress wife, Sharon Tate, and four friends were slaughtered in circumstances that displayed some of the hallmarks of a ritual killing. One person, a caretaker, was shot dead in his car, another was clubbed to death in the house, two were found on the lawn and Sharon Tate was stabbed repeatedly, her body mutilated, after pleading in vain to be spared to have her baby. The following day, Leo Labianca and his wife, who were neighbours of Polanski and Tate, were murdered in a similar fashion. Significantly, the word "Pig" was found written in blood on Sharon Tate's front door, and the phrase "Death to Pigs" was left on the Labiancas' refrigerator door.

By 3 December 1969 several members of a hippie commune had been arrested and charged with the slayings. One, the suspected ringleader, was a bearded, semi-literate, 34-year-old hippie named Charles Manson. The others included Charles "Tex" Watson, aged 24, and three young women. They were Patricia Krenwinkle, aged 28, Linda Kasabian, aged 19, and Susan Denise Atkins, aged 21. Atkins was detained with Manson at the commune headquarters in Death Valley while the others were variously tracked down in Texas, Alabama and New Hampshire. A fifth person, Lesley van Houten, aged 19, was arrested a few days later.

The group to which they belonged was known as the Manson Family. Manson had originally moved, with his following, from the run-down Haight-Ashbury district of San Francisco to a disused film location near Los Angeles known as Spahn Ranch. From there, he and about 20 hippies had transported themselves to two primitive miner's cabins in Death Valley, where they set up residence. The girls either went naked or were clad only in bikini bottoms and the group practised free sex – Manson having directed them that he was a father who knew that it was good to make love. They travelled around the locality in an old bus and raised money, when they needed it, by begging.

All were under the complete domination of Manson, of whom one of the accused, Susan Atkins, said after her arrest, "Our leader is a very beautiful man. We belong to him, not to ourselves." They believed him to be an incarnation of God and the Devil and followed his philosophy that the two are one and the same and that there is, therefore, no such thing as good or evil. Killing another human being was acceptable because it merely liberated the soul.

Manson is alleged to have singled out the Tate residence because he had a grudge against a former tenant, record producer Terry Melcher, the son of the singer Doris Day. It was claimed that he instructed his followers to kill everyone in the house. Atkins, Krenwinkle, van Houten and Watson cut telephone and electricity lines and entered the Benedict Canyon estate while Kasabian, who at the time was five months pregnant, kept watch. Watson shot the caretaker as he was returning to the property in his car and the others killed the occupants of the house.

It seems that Manson's youthful disciples followed his commands to go out and kill without question. They believed that he represented the Second Coming, that he possessed superhuman capabilities and that everything he said and did was beyond criticism. By following him they were above and beyond the law.

On 7 March 1970 Linda Kasabian gave birth in prison. Meanwhile, Manson faced a total of nine charges of murder. He and the women were found guilty on all counts

in January 1971. Charles "Tex" Watson was sentenced only for the murder of the caretaker. They were all given the death penalty in March of that year and placed on Death Row. During the trial there were interventions by President Nixon and at least one lawyer went missing and was found murdered. The death sentence was later commuted to life imprisonment. Manson was still serving this life sentence in Corcoran State Prison, California, when he died following a heart attack, on 19 November 2017, aged 83. Linda Kasabian eventually turned state's evidence in exchange for immunity. Charles Tex Watson escaped the death sentence because of a change in the law in California, but remains in Mule Creek prison, having been denied parole some 13 times. Despite this, he has managed to father 4 children with his ex-wife during conjugal visits, has become a minister, and earned a business degree.

Above: Atkins, Krenwinkle and van Houten before sentencing in a Los Angeles court.

"If you believe in the second coming of Christ, M. is he who has come to save ... in killing someone physically you are only releasing the soul. Life has no boundaries and death is only an illusion. In the word 'kill' the only thing that dies is the ego."

Letter from Susan Atkins, convicted member of Charles Manson's cult commune, 22 February, 1970

ANTON SZANDOR LAVEY AND MADDALENA STRADIVARI

Circus artist, keyboard player and police photographer may appear unlikely qualifications for the founder of a Satanic movement, but the self-styled Anton Szandor LaVey had been a lion tamer and a professional calliopist before turning his San Francisco home into the headquarters of the First Church of Satan in 1966 and advertising himself in the telephone directory under "Churches: Satanist".

LaVey had also dabbled in palmistry but that was the extent of his previous ventures into the occult.

Nonetheless he set about attracting attention to himself as the "High Priest of Satanism", complete with black robes, shaven head, beard and pentangle. His home was decorated in black, an altar was installed and complemented with black candles, incense, swords and other devices. Such was the initial impact of his public relations exercise that he was invited to play the role of the Devil in *Rosemary's Baby*, a cult film of the 1970s. During the 1970s and 1980s, his cult spread across America and even crossed the Atlantic, attracting a group of disciples who were largely comprised of well-educated men between the ages of 30 and 40. Among them was the popular entertainer, Sammy Davis Junior. Membership of the Church of Satan has always been difficult to assess, not least because of the secrecy attached to the organization and the fear of persecution among its members, but the figure has been put at more than 5,000 in the USA alone.

LaVey's greatest claim to posterity lies in his book *The Satanic Bible*, which became a standard source of practical and theological reference for Satanists – all of whom, in essence, attempt to turn morality on its head with the notions that good is bad and bad is good, and that malevolence is to be applauded and benevolence denigrated. The official satanic line is, predictably, less clear-cut. It espouses hedonism by following Aleister Crowley's maxim "To do what thou wilt shall be the whole of the law", which allows for the gratification of man's basic nature and adopts a strongly anarchic, anti-establishment line. On the other hand it vehemently denies entering into the arena of child abuse or ritual killing.

The sexual component of ritual is prominent and one of the essential ingredients of LaVey's service is a naked virgin draped across the altar. Invariably the argument follows that the energy released by sexual activity is essential for the darker aspects of magic to be properly released. Of course, not all of LaVey's converts have been men. One of the more celebrated converts from the world of entertainment was the late Jayne Mansfield who, with her lover Sam Brody, was killed in a car crash. Rumour circulated that some nine months earlier, LaVey had not only put a curse on Brody but warned Mansfield that her continuing association with him would result in fatal consequences.

Women are also known to take a prominent role in satanic activities elsewhere. The lissom, and frequently semi-clothed, figure of Maddalena Stradivari regularly adorns the pages of newspapers when one of the 70 or so occult sects in Italy comes into the public spotlight. Stradivari is a member of *I Spiriti Liberi*, a sexually-oriented cult that carries out its rituals in remote caves in the hills to the south of Rome.

Under the tutelage of her grandmother, Stradivari claims to have lost her virginity at the age of 16 to a satanic high priest. She holds the view that sexual intercourse is an essential ingredient of Satanic ritual, although she asserts that anal rather than vaginal sex provides a more positive stimulus to raising the darker spirits.

Most Satanists will acknowledge that the raising of malevolent entities is an extremely dangerous pursuit and may result in malaise or other affliction, if not worse. There may or may not be an element of truth in this, but it is undoubtedly part of the hype encouraging the view that Satanic worship is an exclusive matter giving great power to those who indulge in its practices. To what extent the actual worship involves drinking blood, burning crucifixes, levelling curses and a host of other alleged malpractices will perhaps always be clothed in mystery, for that is part of the attraction of satanic worship.

Opposite: LaVey claimed he had had a brief affair with Marilyn Monroe, but this was disputed by those who knew her.

SATANISM TODAY

There is an unhealthy and burgeoning cultic interest in the pursuit of evil – that which by convention has been referred to as Satanism. What emerged in the glare of publicity surrounding Charles Manson was not new, nor did it mark the end of the story.

The practice of black arts has continued, though in varying shades. At the extreme end of the spectrum is violence, either self-inflicted or unleashed on others, as demonstrated by the slaughter of Sharon Tate and her friends and neighbours during the hippie era. Black Magic is practised by an unknown number of individuals and small groups. It is, for example, an open secret that Aleister Crowley's occult sect, *Ordo Templi Orientis*, is still active in Britain and the USA. It is also remarkably easy to obtain works describing Satanic rituals in many major bookshops. Aleister Crowley's *Book of the Law* is currently available in a handy pocket-sized volume. Early in 1996, an eccentric royal stalker named Wagner was seen waving a placard depicting a portrait of Queen Elizabeth II with the number 666 – the biblical mark of the Great Beast – pasted across her forehead. These are just some of the outward signs.

To what extent modern Satanism can be linked with child abuse is yet to be determined, but the notion of infant sacrifice to the darker ranks of God is as old as history. The best that can be said is that there continues to be much claim and counter-claim.

It has been calculated that about 10 per cent of all occultists are Satanists, which would mean that there are roughly 10,000 to 20,000 Satanists in Britain, most of whom are men in their twenties and thirties. Not all, of course, are of the calibre of Charles Manson. At the opposite end of the spectrum one finds faintly ludicrous individuals whose evil rests more in the potential than the deed. Such a man is John Kilminster – a furniture maker, local chess devotee and member of his town Conservative Association – who contrived to found the English Church of Satan. He recruited its members through the local paper and convened the first meeting in the local Little Chef restaurant. To new recruits he offered, among other boons, a do-it-yourself training on becoming a werewolf.

It transpired that Kilminster's knowledge of diabolism was virtually non-existent and that his cult membership was largely made up of middle-aged men, whose first interest was less the worship of Lucifer than the possibility of free sex. A small number of women also joined the cult. Kilminster, a married man from Northampton who managed to keep his activities remarkably well hidden from his wife, seems chiefly to have been concerned with finding means to satisfy his libido and delivering devilish homespun rhetoric punctuated by cries of "Hail Satan". Like Anton Szandor LaVey in the USA, Kilminster transformed his daytime workshop into an after-dark satanic temple, complete with black draped altar, black candles, incense and pentangles. One of his favourite rituals was "playing dead" in a coffin while cult members, naked beneath black cloaks, pranced around awaiting his resurrection. This evolved, as the evening wore on, to what the balding and bearded Kilminster entitled "A Celebration of Lust".

At his trial for drug possession, in December 1995, Kilminster admitted having had sex with two cult members, and one ex-member with the cult name Shiva. He was, allegedly, so besotted with Shiva that he had made threatening calls to her when she left his group. She claimed that he had laced her drinks with methadone to make her more compliant. It transpired that Kilminster had spiked members' drinks with supposedly aphrodisiac drugs, the quaintly named *Red Rooster* for the men and *Lady Passion* for the women.

Less comical is 36-year-old Keith Bramble, who became convinced that he was the devil incarnate and used his supernatural powers during a ten-year period during which he terrorized and robbed his wealthy neighbours in the Home Counties. Bramble was described as a career criminal who had earned

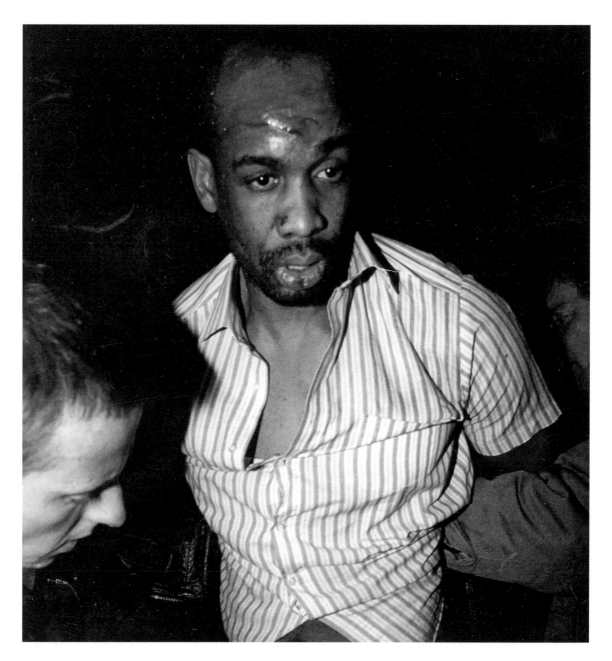

more than £1,000,000 from crime. He used the fear of diabolism to intimidate his victims and made claims that he was invulnerable to prosecution.

Hollywood has done much to export the lurid image of Satanism with such films as the *Omen/Damien* series. Video "nasties" have played their part in influencing vulnerable members of society and some pop and rock groups have incorporated satanic concepts into their songs and videos.

Above: Keith Bramble, 'Britain's Most Dangerous Burglar', during his arrest in 1994.

LEADERS

When reading accounts of some of the extraordinary events involving religious cults that have taken place in recent decades – such as mass suicides, lethal gas attacks, bomb outrages – most observers are bound to frame at least one question: what is the influence, the source of power, that overwhelms apparently normal and intelligent individuals so utterly that they are driven to accept extremes of behaviour?

That the individuals who inspire religious cults possess some intrinsic factor in their personalities that sets them apart from others is undeniable. That almost all those who inspire religious cults are men is perhaps no coincidence. People who have come into direct contact with such latter-day messiahs and gurus all speak of magnetic or mesmeric personalities to which the acolyte rapidly succumbs. Yet, in terms of physical appearance, age, background and intellect, there would appear to be little common ground between cult leaders.

A question that might be posed by a psychiatrist examining some of the extreme deeds perpetrated under the heading of the "messiah phenomena" is whether it is the guru or the followers who are more deranged. Was it the leaders of the Temple du Soleil, Luc Jouret and Joseph Di Mambro, alone who were disturbed when they encouraged dozens of their followers to arrange themselves into star-shaped patterns, swallow drugs and then commit self-immolation, or was it principally the disciples who were mentally unstable?

TRUMPETERS
OF DOOM

The founder of the Jehovah's Witnesses movement, which now claims at least three million members worldwide, about a 100,000 of them in Britain, was born in Pittsburgh, Pennsylvania, to parents who were deeply committed Presbyterians.

At the age of 11 Charles Taze Russell left full-time education and entered the family retail-clothing business with his father – his mother having died in 1861. During his formative years he switched between various Christian sects, first joining the Congregational Church and then the Seventh-Day Adventists, having also dabbled in eastern mysticism.

From the age of 18, in an atmosphere of the Christian fundamentalism that had invaded the USA, he became convinced that the apocalypse and the second coming were imminent. He articulated a belief that Christ had returned to Earth, as an unseen presence, in 1874. This, he claimed, fell into line with certain prophecies contained in the Books of Daniel and Revelation, "...and I, Daniel, alone saw the vision: for the men that were with me saw not the vision; but a great quaking fell upon them, so that they fled to hide themselves", (Daniel 10:7).

To prepare humanity for this event and to spread the word, he launched a magazine, *Zion's Watchtower* and *Herald of Christ's Presence*, in 1879. The title was to be superseded by the well-known *Watchtower* and *Awake* publications that continue to be taken from door to door by evangelical members of his sect. With the help of his wife, Maria, Russell produced a steady stream of doom-laden pamphlets and distributed them to a gullible public through a devoted and expanding team of acolytes. Russell had extracted elements from the beliefs of other Doomsday adherents and added homespun ingredients of his own. Little of what he espoused was original, but he proclaimed that any who disagreed with his dictates would be destined for annihilation. In contrast, at Armageddon, the true faithful would be spared – 144,000 of them being airlifted to Paradise and the remainder left to populate the newly cleansed Earth.

Russell had joined the other evangelicals in the hazardous game of prediction, his success coming largely through the efficient distribution of his publications for which he had employed his undoubted marketing skills. Christ, he alleged, had communicated a warning to him that the world would end in 1914. Others, however, had succumbed to this pitfall and been made to look foolish when dates came and went and the Earth kept turning more or less as normal. Russell found a scapegoat for his failure in the unlikely form of the Great Pyramid of Cheops at El Giza near Cairo, Egypt. The dimensions of this remarkable construction have been measured with great precision – it is 230 metres (2,475 feet) square by 147 metres (482 feet) high – but at the time they were subject to debate. By converting the measurements into a time period but then claiming to have revised the figures, Russell was able to massage the date of the end of the world to suit himself. Toward the year of 1914, when the first rumblings of total disaster did not appear on the horizon, he began to suggest that the El Giza measurements might need checking again.

Russell died in 1916, with the Earth shaken but not wholly stirred by the events of 1914. He had appointed no official successor. Meanwhile, many of his more ardent followers – who had not heeded his cautionary words – had sold off their houses and other possessions.

THE JUDGE

Russell was to be succeeded, after much infighting, by Joseph Franklin Rutherford, a New York attorney who had represented the Witnesses in several lawsuits and who took the self-styled title of "The Judge". He and other members were arrested during World War I and charged with sedition because of his pacifist stance against priests who were supporting the USA's involvement in the war. Rutherford received a 20-year sentence but was released after less than a year. At this juncture the date of Armageddon had been put back to

1925 and the by now familiar sale of goods and houses reached fever pitch as the date approached. Although the absence of doom brought some opprobrium, the Witnesses' fortunes rallied during the Depression of the 1930s. Rutherford was able to purchase a property in California that was to be held in trust for the elders of the Old Testament, who he proclaimed were due to return to Earth. He also became increasingly dismissive of other branches of the Christian faith and developed such a despotic manner that his wife and son abandoned him. During this time he indulged himself in a luxury property in San Diego.

The name Jehovah's Witnesses was not actually introduced until 1931, when Rutherford decided that it would provide a suitable title for the society members. It was also at this time that he urged the sect members to ignore federal laws regarding payment of taxes and doorstep canvassing. He died leaving the Witnesses exposed to an unparalleled level of attack from Church and State.

Above: Jehovah's Witnesses graduate at the Yankee Stadium, New York City, 1950.

CHARLES MANSON

The self-styled "God and Satan" achieved notoriety not so much as the founder of a cult but rather as the organizer of a brutal, ritualized slaying amid the glitter of the Hollywood film world. His crime was made all the more sensational because one of his victims was the pregnant and glamorous wife of a celebrated film director.

Charles Manson was born in 1935. He was an under-achiever at school who ended his education as a semi-literate dropout with a growing chip on his shoulder. Until the late 1960s, he remained virtually unknown. In his 34th year, when free love and alternative lifestyles were very much the trend among California's youth, he presented an almost hypnotic appearance and manner, with black hippie locks, a beard and dark penetrating eyes. In the years before the trial that brought him to prominence he was living in Haight-Ashbury, a rundown suburb of San Francisco that had become popular with the dropouts of the city, and it was among these squalid surroundings that he first began to attract a band of devotees.

His philosophy was simple and crude, effectively echoing the hedonistic maxims of black magicians such as Aleister Crowley. He espoused the belief that all human beings are God and the Devil at one and the same time. His bizarre theories included the notion that to kill a human being is acceptable because one is killing only a part of one's self. His followers, he claimed, were above the law because they were divinely guided – familiar rhetoric that was to be emulated by many other cult leaders in the decades that followed.

Manson became fascinated with Black Magic and achieved almost total psychological power over his flock through instilling a belief in his supernatural powers. What Manson ordered was done without question. Those who knew him well spoke of a moody personality and of slow, deliberate, physical motions. He also possessed a prodigious sexual appetite and gained a reputation among his young female acolytes

Right: During his 1970 trial, Manson was asked, "Are you insane, Charlie?". He replied, "It all depends on your point of view."

as an accomplished lover. To facilitate his needs in this area, but also to extend his overall control, he promoted the view that the women of the commune were his personal property. Other members were openly welcome to share them with him but only on the understanding that, by doing so, they became Manson's property too. Thus he ordered the girls of the commune to have sex, as and when necessary, with any man that he wanted to recruit.

Manson preached a gospel of hate. He showed an almost total loathing of society in general – of blacks, whites, the establishment, the judicial system, of the affluence that pervaded California and, particularly, the Hollywood movie industry. Yet while he placed no value on human life, he advocated extreme respect for animal life, which he regarded as sacrosanct. The Death Valley commune that he controlled was, at times, infested with snakes and other pests yet he would allow none to be killed.

THE KILLINGS

On 9 August 1969, he instructed four of his followers, a man and three women, one pregnant, to go to the home of Roman Polanski and carry out the brutal killing of five innocent people, one of whom was also pregnant, and then to conduct a copycat killing of two next-door neighbours the following day.

A number of bizarre reasons were put forward as to why he ordered these killings. Manson, it was claimed, wanted to start a revolution of blacks against whites, and had deliberately orchestrated events to make it seem as if black militants had carried out the attacks. Others claimed that he was encouraged by the lyrics

of a Beatles song or that his motive was revenge against a previous tenant of the rented estate where Polanski and his wife lived. It was also claimed that Polanski had been involved in some kind of drug-related orgy that got out of hand, an accusation that Polanski strongly refuted.

THE AFTERMATH

Manson was arrested, along with a member of his cult, at the Death Valley commune in October 1969. He claimed that he had done nothing more than mete out punishment for, and liberation from, an affluent lifestyle and insisted that he was the reincarnation of God, Jesus and Satan. Along with four others, he was indicted for murder in Los Angeles on 8 December. A little more than a month later he went on hunger strike, demanding that he should conduct his own defence and that the hearing should be postponed. He was forced to accept legal representation and the trial finally opened on 24 July 1970. On 12 January 1971, Manson was convicted of first-degree murder and on 30 March was sentenced to death, placed on Death Row, and remained there until his sentence was commuted to life imprisonment.

Charles Manson stands, arguably, among the most evil-minded cult leaders of recent times. Others of a similar persuasion may have been involved in ritual murder, but not under such spectacular circumstances or involving such high-profile victims. From the confines of prison, he wrote songs and launched a bizarre commercial-cum-atonement enterprise, an exercise video. According to his promoter, Fred Zalemond, it was "an expression of Charlie's regret for the lives taken". "Now," said Zalemond, "he's saving lives by protecting people from heart attacks and strokes." Manson died, still a prisoner, in 2017.

Left: The body of pregnant actress Sharon Tate is removed from her home in Beverly Hills, California, 1969.

LAFAYETTE RONALD HUBBARD

Few individuals in fringe religious movements have captured public interest in the way of L. Ron Hubbard, founder of the Church of Scientology, not least because his is among the biggest and most affluent of twentieth-century sects.

L. Ron Hubbard was born in 1911 at Tilden, Nebraska, but was brought up in Montana in a close-knit family. Theirs was not, as has been promoted in Scientology literature, a life on a wealthy cattle ranch belonging to his grandfather. Hubbard's father, Harry, was briefly an enlisted officer in the United States Navy and on two occasions, the first being in 1927, the teenage Ron travelled with his mother to Guam to visit his father, who was serving on a shore station. L. Ron Hubbard attended George Washington University and studied molecular physics. He left without graduating and spent much of his time writing mediocre science fiction, adventure screenplays and magazine stories. During World War II he followed his father's footsteps into the Navy, where he pursued an equally uneventful service. Claims that he was a war hero were subsequently elaborated by the Scientologist media machine, which implied that his official war records had been altered in some way. He never saw enemy action and ended his active service being treated for a duodenal ulcer in a naval hospital.

His first marriage ended when he left his wife and their two children and went through an illegal wedding ceremony with Sara Elizabeth Northrup, the former mistress of one of his friends. The friend, Jack Parsons, was employed as a rocket scientist but was also into the darker aspects of magic and Satanism and was a disciple of the English magician, Aleister Crowley. It was through Parsons that Hubbard developed a personal interest in magical cults.

Amid a torrent of accusations of cruelty, Hubbard left his second wife and abducted their daughter, Alexis, for several months while a deal was struck with Sara. By this time measurable amounts of money were coming into the Foundation accounts and, away from the problems of his personal life, Hubbard was riding high.

Above: L. Ron Hubbard and his Electrometer.

THE CHURCH OF SCIENTOLOGY

Hubbard developed a new slant on his craze for off-beat "science of the mind" by developing Scientology, an esoteric jumble of theories gathered from science fiction, theology and physics, the details of which were, from the outset, shrouded in secrecy. It was from this quasi-scientific base that he invented his peculiar style of religion, which became known as the Church of Scientology. Essentially, Scientologists argue that the earthly body is a temporary vehicle for a powerful entity known as a Thetan, but that the effectiveness of each Thetan, which has been cruising the galaxy in one form or another for about 75 million years, can be diminished by implants known as Engrams. These originate from a variety of sources but their presence can be conveniently measured by an electrical device (invented by Hubbard) called an E-meter. These Engrams can then be eliminated by psychotherapy and confession, a process that Scientologists refer to as "auditing".

One of the first major incidents of open dissent against Hubbard's activities came when, in 1959, his eldest son, Ron Junior, or "Nibs", turned against him and made a very public declaration that his father was insane. Hubbard himself made allegations that his daughter Alexis had probably been fathered by Jack Parsons. At the end of the 1960s, he married his third wife, Mary Sue.

"The least free person is the person who cannot reveal his own acts and who protests the revelation of the improper acts of others. On such people will be built a future political slavery."

L. Ron Hubbard

RETIREMENT

In 1967, Hubbard turned his attention to developing a private "navy". Having resigned as head of the Church of Scientology, though keeping control of its assets, he founded Sea Org, a maritime branch of Scientology, complete with three vessels that he crewed with disciples and sailed around the Caribbean and the Mediterranean. By this time he was surrounding himself with young, largely female, acolytes – known as Commodore's Messengers – who were exclusively at his beck and call and who came to represent the inner court that gradually took over the reins of power as Hubbard grew toward old age. He returned to dry land in 1975, suffered the first of two heart attacks and settled, surrounded by trusted Messengers, on a ranch property near Palm Springs, Florida.

Tragedy struck in 1976 when Hubbard's second son, Quentin, committed suicide because he realized that his homosexuality would not be tolerated in the Church of Scientology. Hubbard suffered his second heart attack in 1978 and, by this time, was increasingly convinced that the Federal authorities were engaged in undercover surveillance of the Scientologists. In 1980 his wife, Mary Sue, and other members of the sect were involved in a bizarre bugging and theft operation. Large quantities of material were stolen from government offices. This resulted in arrests and jail sentences. Mary Sue Hubbard began a one-year jail term in 1983 after a series of appeals had failed.

In 1980, L. Ron Hubbard disappeared into virtual obscurity with a small coterie of Messengers and, despite failing health, enjoyed a luxurious lifestyle that was funded from the Church of Scientology coffers. He suffered a fatal stroke in 1986.

DIANETICS

One of the major breakthroughs in Hubbard's career came in 1949, when he published an article in a magazine called *Astounding Science Fiction* in which he expounded the theory of what he described as "Dianetics, a science of thought". Following the success of this piece he wrote his first best-selling book on Dianetics, which explained how to overcome an assortment of psychosomatic conditions, from arthritis to alcoholism, and founded his Hubbard Dianetics and Research Foundations.

THE SWAMIS OF HARE KRISHNA

The first guru to carry the Hindu Krishna cult to the USA was an elderly retired businessman, Prabhupada, who had spent most of his working life running a chemical plant in Calcutta, India.

In 1965, at the age of 69, he emigrated to the USA with a one-way ticket provided by a sponsor, a trunkful of religious books and little more in the way of possessions or money. His vocation was to bring an understanding of the values of Krishna devotion to the Western world.

In the early years of the century, Prabhupada qualified as a graduate of philosophy, economics and English. In 1922, he became attracted to the Krishna revivalist movement, which was gaining popularity in India. During the years before and after World War II he set about the task of translating a considerable number of religious texts into English as part of an instruction from his own

Swami "to carry Krishna consciousness to the West" until, in 1959, he became a *sanyassi*, a religious ascetic who relinquishes material things to pursue his faith.

Once established in New York, Prabhupada rapidly gained a flock among the intellectual hippie community, who were urgently seeking new spiritual horizons. His regular lectures became well-known, offering a rigid code of morality and a fundamentalist doctrine that

---

Above: Hare Krishna supports in front of Prabhupada's golden palace.

dismissed, as unnecessary, stimulants including coffee, tea, alcohol and sex for gratification, while insisting on strict vegetarianism and the renouncing of many worldly values. So successful was his mission that within a year he had founded ISKCON (the International Society for Krishna Consciousness). In 1968, he established an ISKCON headquarters in England, first in London and then in a fine country residence located near Watford, Hertfordshire, that had been owned by George Harrison (of the Beatles), and sold at a knock-down price. By 1973, the original New York base had expanded to 68 regional headquarters spread throughout the Western world with approximately 3,000 fully paid-up disciples. Throughout the time of growth, Swami Prabhupada travelled extensively, promoting Krishna consciousness worldwide until his death in 1977.

Anticipating that he had not long to live, he established a so-called International Governing Body Commission. This was, in reality, a cumbersome title for a cadre of 29 young intellectual dropouts. Regrettably, he left no clear mandate for succession to his position of leadership. The Hare Krishna movement, as it came to be popularly known, was left sitting on the business empire Prabhupada had created. It possessed a substantial bank balance but no Director of Corporate Affairs. Left in his wake was a clique of young street-wise governors. They had a surfeit of ambition but little experience of business. Almost immediately, 11 of the 29 members of the commission issued the unsubstantiated claim that Swami Prabhupada had made a death-bed announcement that they were to carry the succession forward. Their spokesman was Keith Ham, otherwise known as Kirtanananda, who had been one of the original American disciples and the first of Prabhupada's own sanyassis. He took control and instigated a tough regime, effectively setting up his own Krishna movement, New Vrindavan, based around a superb marble temple that he had built, more or less with slave labour from devotees, on a site in West Virginia. From there he issued directives to ISKCON worldwide.

THE POWER STRUGGLE

From the time of Kirtanananda's accession, infighting resulted in a series of murders, which severely rocked the movement; these incidents included shootings and a decapitation. A British-based breakaway group under the leadership of an oversexed LSD dependant named

Above: Swami Prabhupada at Valencay Castle in France, July 1979.

James Immel, who was also known as Jayatirtha, survived from 1982 until he was beheaded by one of his own followers, John Tiernan, in 1987. Like Immel, Tiernan was a frequent user of the drug LSD, who probably committed the assassination while tripping. He stated that he had carried out the killing in protest at Immel's plans to set up a personal harem – which ran contrary to Prabhupada's somewhat misogynistic stance on women in ISKCON. Tiernan had joined the movement in 1975 and had taken the name Navanita Cora. After conviction for murder he was committed to a mental institution.

Today, little is published about the organization's leaders. One of the international swamis, Bhakti Svarupa Damodara, died on 2 October 2006 at Kolkata in India, the victim of a grenade attack. Another of the current leaders in the UK, H. H. Lokenath, was in the news in October 2006, when his van overturned in an accident and he suffered cuts to his left arm.

SWAMI RAJNEESH

Bhagwan Shree Rajneesh was born Rajneesh Chandra Mohan, the eldest of 13 siblings, into a middle-class family in India. He was raised by his grandparents, who are said to have spoiled him. Having completed his basic schooling, he entered the University of Jabalpur and obtained a degree in philosophy.

Rajneesh was considered a difficult student but went on to lecture in philosophy for the next 10 years before taking up the life of a spiritual teacher, or guru. He became recognized as an accomplished intellectual, a progressive writer and a poet, although he claimed to disagree with the principle of intellectual thought and preferred the route of meditation and mysticism.

Once he had appointed himself as a guru he quickly attracted a following of young converts, who became captivated by his magnetic personality. He taught meditation and total, unthinking devotion – effectively a form of religious brainwashing. In common with other cultic leaders, he also used his hypnotic influence to satisfy a sexual appetite. He claimed that the act of sex opened a doorway to the divine. Procreation under this influence, he further claimed, would establish a generation of devotees to be reared and nurtured under the communal ideals that pervaded the 1970s and 1980s. Within this environment he proclaimed that good and bad were indistinguishable other than through the values placed on behaviour by distorted human principles.

THE CULT GROWS

By the early 1970s, Rajneesh had settled in Bombay, where he made his religious headquarters. He received the adoration of many Western dropouts and seekers of alternative faith. Their travels provided a cover for the collection of drugs, which were then peddled in Europe. The proceeds of these sales were then funnelled back to swell the Bhagwan's bank accounts. He also managed to attract considerable antagonism on the sub-continent for his hostility and derogation of others, including Gandhi and Mother Teresa of Calcutta. His self-styled title of Bhagwan (Master of the Vagina) and his overseeing of naked, sexually-charged romps on the seashore brought more local disfavour. In 1974, he relocated the cult to

Poona, where acolytes dressed in rose-coloured robes and radiated joy, at least for the benefit of reporters and television cameras. Less overt were the encounter exercises – where acolytes were encouraged to release their frustrations by attacking each other – and the sexual meditation sessions, which proceeded under the Rajneesh philosophy of perfection through free love and total loss of sexual inhibition.

By the late 1970s, Rajneesh was under investigation by the Indian authorities after incidents of attempted insurance fraud. He also faced charges of tax evasion. He made a timely escape to the United States and settled his commune, to the concern of the local authorities, on a ranch adjacent to the small town of Antelope in Wasco County. It had cost him not less than $6,000,000. Within a short space of time the cult was wielding enormous influence in the district while Rajneesh continued to control his flock using a cocktail of mind-bending, intimidation and brute force.

"The wicked is ruling his kingdom clad in silver and gold, while the virtuous lives in the forest, wearing the bark of trees."

The Mahabrata

Opposite: A smiling Bhagwan Shree Rajneesh.

THE BUBBLE BURSTS

Rajneesh had by now become largely reclusive, delivering all his directives through an Indian secretary, whose given cult name was Ma Anand Sheela. He continued to live an ostentatiously luxurious existence, travelling everywhere by Rolls-Royce while his followers existed in squalor and deprivation. The bubble burst in 1985 when Rajneesh fell out with his most senior lieutenants and with Ma Anand Sheela. Becoming aware that his protective entourage in Rajneeshpuram was fast evaporating, he tried to escape to Bermuda but was intercepted at Charlotte-Douglas International airport in Carolina, where his private jet had stopped to re-fuel. He was arrested, jailed on a charge of fraud involving fake visa applications, convicted and then deported to India after making a payment of $400,000. The Indian authorities refused him residence so he flew on, first to Nepal and then on a globe-trotting trek that kept him on the move through various countries until 1987. He eventually returned to India and was allowed to retire to his old residence at Poona. He remained there plagued by ill-health, which he blamed on the American authorities, until his death at the age of 58. Various claims were put forward that he had been poisoned but it is also considered possible that he died of AIDS – as did certain members of his senior entourage. As an indication of his wealth and power, at the peak of his influence Rajneesh is said to have owned a fleet of more than 90 Rolls-Royces, four private aircraft, a fleet of buses and an impressive private arsenal.

"Roll on your stomach so that your bare navel touches the earth... press your body close to the earth, blend into it and recapture the moment of childhood when you pressed yourself on your mother's breast."

Swami Rajneesh, from his interpretation of the Sufi Whirling Meditation technique.

Right: Adoring followers hoping to greet Rajneesh as he arrives for a press conference at his home in California, 1984.

THE MESSIAH OF WACO

Vernon Howell, better known as David Koresh, was the leader of the ill-fated cult known as the Branch Davidians, a role which he took over from a fellow Texan and founder of the Branch Davidians, Ben Roden. Koresh perished in the fire that engulfed the sect compound at Waco in Texas at about noon on 19 April 1993.

To his followers he was the new Messiah, preaching an apocalyptic message based largely on the prophetic texts of the biblical Books of Daniel and Revelation. To the public at large he appeared to be a power-crazed, sexually charged lunatic.

As an adolescent, Howell had two obsessive interests, the electric guitar and the Bible. Following in his mother's steps, he was baptized into the local church of the Seventh-Day Adventists in 1979. He was struck off the rolls shortly afterward for his dissenting behaviour – he argued that the sect had become compromised from its original purpose. Implacably committed to the idea of the second coming of Christ, he joined the Branch Davidians at Mount Carmel in 1981. He enjoyed a sexual relationship with Lois, the 67-year-old widow of Ben Roden, who was now the leader of the Branch Davidians and who declared that the re-named David Koresh was to be her successor.

THE MARRYING KIND

In 1984, Koresh married Rachel Jones, the 14-year-old daughter of another Branch Davidian member, Perry Jones. In January 1985 he and Rachel, who was by now pregnant, travelled to Israel, where it was later claimed that he received confirmation of his messianic calling. Lois Roden died in 1986 but her son, George, disputed Koresh's claim to the leadership of the cult. In the same year Koresh also took a second wife, Rachel's 12-year-old sister, Michelle. Koresh took a further three wives in 1987 – all, he said, according to the instructions given to him by God. By the end of 1988, Roden had been declared insane and committed to a state hospital and David Koresh was the leader of the Branch Davidians at Mount Carmel.

It was his experience in Israel in 1985 that was to provide his defence. He claimed that he was the recipient of God's final message, the so-called Seventh Seal, and

that he was, therefore, the appointed seventh messenger of the Book of Revelation: 10:7:

But in the days of the voice of the seventh angel, when he shall begin to sound, the mystery of God should be finished, as he hath declared to his servants, the prophets.

Koresh had gained this mystical information having been transported briefly to heaven and transformed from into the apocalyptic "rider of the white horse".

CHILDREN OF GOD

Koresh decided to keep the outside world at bay and, quoting instructions from the New Testament to endorse his actions, stockpiled weapons at Mount Carmel. Branch members who survived Waco claimed that Koresh was justified in doing this as he was running a legitimate gun business. In the summer of 1989, Koresh declared an extraordinary edict: all commune members were to separate from their wives and partners and become celibate, following the recommendations of St Paul. Koresh, being semi-divine, on the other hand, gave himself the absolute right to have sexual relationships with any of the female members of the cult that he chose. He was, like others of his kind, procreating "Children of God" in a sacred act that had nothing to do with libido or lust.

Koresh came to believe that the Branch Davidians, in their thousands, would emigrate to Israel, where at some time in the future a final conflict would be played out and he would be killed. He gained his conviction from passages in Isaiah. Unfortunately, they did not warn him of events that were to take place at Waco in April 1993.

.

Opposite: A 1981 photo of David Koresh, taken at the Mount Carmel compound that was later the site of the infamous standoff.

THE RESURRECTION

At the time of the fire, Koresh claimed an indeterminate number of wives (two of whom were pregnant) and at least 12 children, all of whom perished. His surviving followers believed that he would be resurrected to a position of majesty and glory on 13 December 1996 – 1,335 days after his death, and again on 6 August 1999 – in accordance with a prophetic utterance in the Book of Daniel: "Blessed is he that waiteth, and cometh to the thousand three hundred and five and thirty days. But go thy way till the end be: for thou shalt rest, and stand in thy lot at the end of the days." (Daniel: 12.9/12/13). Undaunted, they believe that Koresh will reincarnate and lead them to a new Branch Davidian utopia at some undisclosed point in the future.

"And I saw another angel ascending from the east having the seal of the living God; and he cried with a loud voice to the four angels, to whom it was given to hurt the Earth and the sea, saying, Hurt not the earth, neither the sea, nor the trees till we have sealed the servants of our Gods in their foreheads. And I heard the number of them which were sealed: and there were sealed a hundred and forty four thousand of all the tribes and children of Israel."

Book of Revelation: 7.2–4

DAVID BERG

This extraordinary man only came to notoriety when he was approaching middle age. At the height of his powers he presented an improbable-looking figure, sporting a pot-belly, balding hippie locks and a patriarchal beard.

Until the hippie cult of the late 1960s and 1970s Berg had pursued an uneventful career teaching and evangelizing as a travelling preacher. It was not until he and his impoverished family arrived on the beaches of California to join his mother and her charitable mission for dropouts that he began to attract attention.

Berg created a small but attractive sect, the Teens for Christ movement, which lured hippies with a mixture of protest music, free love-on-the-sand for Jesus, peanut butter sandwiches, dispensed by his mother, and profound opinions about the meaning of existence. He proclaimed an anti-establishment, anti-disciplinarian message that found favour with his rapidly growing band of youthful and unwashed converts and, as in the case of many other comparable gurus, held the loyalty of his acolytes with messages of impending doom for those who did not follow the law according to David Berg. That he possessed a willing and malleable audience was obvious – most of his followers had already deserted homes, jobs and other worldly ties. In the wake of Vietnam, and other horrors of a culture that they perceived as being both imperialistic and materially obsessed, they were content to take up the cross and follow Berg for the sake of a free meal and a life of ease, drugs and spirituality.

One of the most powerful innovations that Berg brought was the combining of religion and pop music, to which he added the ingredients of a hippie appearance, an attractive venue on the balmy Californian shore that was far removed from the seemingly old-fashioned and stuffy confines of orthodox worship and an essentially anti-establishment message. In this he likened himself to his archetypal religious model, Jesus Christ, and his ego blossomed.

THE PROPHET OF THE APOCALYPSE

As the message that Berg was delivering to his followers – now called the Children of God – spread, so he began to adapt and corrupt what had, originally, been fairly harmless. He changed his name to Moses David and proclaimed himself the prophet of the apocalypse. American imperialism would, he asserted to his followers, be the victim of its own godlessness and the only way to escape the wrath of the Almighty was to shelter within a new church in which he would stand at the head. In his increasing delusions of grandeur he was assisted by a young convert, Karen "Maria" Zerby, for whose affections Berg abandoned his wife – although she remained, technically, part of his family and lived under the same roof.

Berg had originally taught the advantages of celibacy but, partly through a wish to justify his own adultery, he began to proclaim the opposite, the notion of free love, to his converts. He confided to them that God had personally instructed him to take a mistress as the symbol of his new church, claiming that his wife, Jane, reflected the old and inadequate faith. At about this time, Berg also became increasingly reclusive and resorted to communicating with his devotees through an endless series of letters. These, predictably, became much sought after and were treated with the reverence of biblical writings, irrespective of the banal, and often prurient, material they contained. Like other would-be Messiahs, such as the English witch, Gerald Gardner, he embellished his remote and rather crude rhetoric by delivering it in a mixture of pseudo-archaic language and idiomatic slang but, increasingly, it became sexually slanted.

THE FAMILY OF LOVE

By 1972, Berg was under investigation by the authorities in the USA and so he quietly left for England, setting up a new headquarters in genteel and leafy suburbia near Bromley, Kent. At this time he practised partner sharing, demanding that the men among his followers offered

Left: David Berg – the orignal 'Jesus Freak'?

him their spouses for his personal entertainment. By 1976, he was preaching free love and anarchy as standard requirements of membership of the Children of God. Sharing was the name of the game since, in Berg's view, it was God, the father of all, who was actually performing the acts of adultery. Two years later, in an effort to maintain a respectable front in the face of increasingly hostile publicity about the apparently salacious activities of the sect, he changed its title from Children of God, giving it the less contentious title of The Family of Love.

SEX FOR JESUS

Through the sale of his literature, Berg was by this time living in some luxury but was obsessed with getting his message to an ever-wider audience. To this end he introduced the concept of "Flirty Fishing", or "FFing" as it came to be dubbed. Women members were, in effect, required to prostitute themselves in clubs, bars and other social meeting places for the sake of recruitment, irrespective of whether they

were married or single. "Sex for Jesus" became the buzz-phrase until the late 1980s, when the spread of AIDS made it unrealistic. Berg spread the sexual promiscuity message to include lesbianism and paedophilia.

Berg became an elusive shadow. There were claims that he had escaped from England to live in southern Europe. He died in 1994. He was eventually exposed to the world at large in a book written by his eldest daughter, Linda, but in his day he used his undoubted charisma and persuasive tongue to seduce and impoverish, spiritually and materially, the lives of thousands of individuals. There exists today a generation of adults, minds confused, parentage unknown, that represents David Berg's most tragic legacy. The Family, meanwhile, continues to attract converts.

"There are no laws against incest in the loving Kingdom of God."

David Berg

SHOKO ASAHARA

There is good reason to believe that 41-year-old Shoko Asahara, a fervent admirer of Adolph Hitler and the Nazi regime, is mentally unstable. He was born in 1955, the son of a tatami-maker, and although only partially blind from birth was sent to a blind school where he was the only pupil with any visual sense at all.

In this respect, he was heavily relied on as a leader by other pupils and the experience may have opened the way to messianic convictions. He also discovered the techniques of manipulating and bullying others.

After he left school, Asahara took up herbalism and acupuncture as a profession but was arrested and convicted for selling fake potions. He went on to found the Heavenly Blessing Association and when this collapsed, in 1982, he founded the equally obscure Aum Divine Wizard Association, which also collapsed. It was after this unprepossessing beginning to his career that he travelled to the Himalayas, where he claimed to have reached the state of perfection, or nirvana, called, in Japanese terms, *satori*. Armed with enlightenment and 10 disciples, he founded the Aum cult in 1987.

Shoko Asahara was a rather improbable-looking leader. He was squat, myopic, had a dark beard and long hippie-style hair, and wore a white jumpsuit and training shoes. To his followers, however, he was the reincarnation of a personality who lived during the twenty-seventh century BC. They knew Asahara as "The Master", a reincarnation of Imhotep, builder of the great step pyramid complex at Sakkara in Egypt. Imhotep was respected as a sage and an accomplished scribe and, after his death, he achieved a virtually mythical status as the son of the creator god, Ptah, with cult centres both at Sakkara and Memphis, where he was revered as the "Great Physician". His cult continued into Roman times but why Asahara took Imhotep as an idol is unclear other than the general belief some Adventists held that, at the millennium, the great pyramid of Giza would opened up and Satan would then emerge to claim his kingdom.

Shoko Asahara based his teachings on a mixture of Buddhism, Hinduism, Egyptian mysticism and New Age philosophies. With such thoughts and promises he began to attract a steady flow of recruits, mainly from among Japan's affluent and intellectual youth. With revenue flowing in from the pockets of devotees he built up a sizeable fortune. In 1989, he moved the main commune of cult members to Kamikuishiki in a remote country district near Mount Fuji. The following year he and 24 other cult members stood for the Japanese parliament but gained virtually no support outside of the cult's own voters. He promptly issued a warning that Mount Fuji was about to erupt. He alone, he asserted, was in a position to save at least some of humanity and prophesied that Aum members would be delivered by spaceship to a new civilization in some far-off galaxy before the day of Armageddon came in 1997. He also began to talk openly, if obscurely, of the use of chemical weapons, including Sarin gas.

GAS ATTACKS

In June 1994, seven people died in the coastal city of Matsumoto after Sarin gas was released in the vicinity of an apartment building where three judges lived. These same judges were poised to rule on a lawsuit brought against Aum. From that moment it seems clear that Shoko Asahara intended to launch a full-scale guerrilla war on the Japanese civilian population. There was another Sarin gas attack, this time against the Tokyo subway system, on 20 March 1995. Many of Shoko Asahara's followers were arrested but he escaped with his wife and six children. When his office was searched after the gas attack, the police discovered 22 pounds of gold bullion and the equivalent of about £5,000,000 in cash. In his absence, one of his most trusted lieutenants, Kenji Takagi, travelled to Tokyo to supervise a public relations damage limitation exercise. At 26, Takagi, a one-time computer engineer, devoted himself to promoting Shoko Asahara's beliefs and to mending fences. This is not an easy task among a population that, in May 1995, received

reports of bags of potentially lethal chemicals being deposited in the men's toilet of another Tokyo station, presumably by Aum members. In February 2004, Shoko Ashara was finally convicted and sentenced to death; his final appeal was rejected in September 2006, and the execution by hanging took place in July 2018.

Above: Shoko Asahara, meditating in India.

"I fully admit that my beliefs are crazy. But sometimes it takes crazy beliefs to achieve perfect freedom and happiness."

Shoko Asahara

THE MESSIAH OF JONESTOWN

In style and motivation, James Jones was little different from so many other slightly mad messiahs but in the way that he brought his cult to its apocalyptic climax he was the first of his kind.

James Thurman Jones was born in 1931 and claimed part white and part Cherokee Indian heritage. Jones attended University in Indianapolis and set up his first evangelic church there at the age of 18, selling South American monkeys to raise the necessary funds. Although he styled himself the Reverend Jim Jones, James Jones was neither

ordained nor had he received any formal training as a pastor. He built up a devoted following by broadcasting a message that contained a mix of political and religious ingredients.

According to Jones's autobiographical diary, he joined the American Communist Party sometime during the early 1950s. He also married Marceline, usually shortened to Marcie, and they built a multiracial family through the adoption of seven children. In 1959, they also had a son, Stephen.

In 1961, Jones received a vision of a holocaust engulfing Indianapolis. At about the same time it was also revealed in *Esquire* magazine that one of the nine safest places on Earth was the Redwood Valley in north California. He therefore decided to uproot and lead his band of 100 followers to the small community of Ukiah, where he built a church, a baptismal swimming pool, a large coach park and a comfortable residence for himself. Although his flock included some white people, it consisted mainly of African-Americans, Asians and Native Americans.

Jones preached a gospel of racial equality that was virtually indistinguishable from Marxism, though with a Christian slant. So successful was the enterprise that he moved to San Francisco, where he ran his People's Temple from an old church in a poor section of the town. He catered mainly to local people, preaching the elimination of class distinction and the end of the oppression of the poor, and sought to prove that people of various backgrounds could live together without conflict.

A short, chubby man who habitually wore tinted glasses and second-hand suits, Jones nevertheless possessed a compelling charisma and as his reputation spread, he began to hold services elsewhere in San Francisco and also further afield in Los Angeles.

In 1971, he purchased an abandoned synagogue on Geary Boulevard in a derelict section of San Francisco that was populated largely by African-Americans. A few months later he bought another property, this time in Los Angeles. Jones was reaping an annual income of over $200,000 by persuading his disciples to hand over money and possessions. He travelled everywhere surrounded by a bodyguard of up to 15 people.

Jones's strategy included the cultivation of leading political figures in San Francisco. He had his followers engage in door-to-door vote catching for those who would help him with his aims, powerful figures who included the State Governor and the mayors of San Francisco and Los Angeles. In turn, he was elected chairman of the San Francisco housing authority, a position that led him to once share the stage with Rosalynn Carter when she opened the San Francisco Democratic Party headquarters in 1976. He was also invited to meet Vice President Walter Mondale.

It was in August 1977 that Jones, already the subject of a hostile press over rumours of extortion, fake healings and death threats to those who left his church, gained permission to take his commune to the Marxist paradise-on-Earth of Guyana. Such was his measure of control that 1,200 people followed him to the jungle commune that was to be named Jonestown. Once there, his rule became increasingly authoritarian. He claimed that rigid discipline was the only way to prepare his flock for the rigours of nuclear holocaust. He had also become increasingly paranoid and deranged. It is said that he believed that the CIA was poisoning his food and that he sometimes imagined that he was Lenin. He frequently spoke with a Russian accent and often gave out dire warnings of impending attack, which were broadcast over the commune loudspeakers. He also spoke of the prospect of suicide.

By the late summer of 1978, Jones had reached the point of no return. He had been warned that a United States Congressman, Leo Ryan, would be visiting the commune along with several members of the press corps to investigate complaints that United States citizens were being effectively imprisoned by the commune against their will. On 18 November, Ryan and his colleagues were executed on Jones's orders as they tried to leave Jonestown. On 20 November, the mass suicide and massacre took place of 911 cult members. Jones, then aged 47, was found among piles of bodies, lying on his back, a bullet wound to his head. His last words are reported to have been, "Mother, Mother, Mother."

20 November 2008 marked the thirtieth anniversary of this man's grotesque death and the massacre that he oversaw. When he died his personal assets were believed to have been well over $5,000,000 and he had left instructions that the vast wealth accumulated by the cult in overseas banks was to be sent to Russia. The Soviet authorities declined his donation. His wife once said of him that he was never a true believer in Christianity but a committed Marxist who had hoped to use Christian fundamentalism to bring potential followers into his orbit, where he could influence them to support his aims.

"Mothers you must keep your children under control. They must die with dignity."

An extract from the final taped exhortations of James Jones.

Opposite: Jim and wife Marceline with their adopted children and Jim's sister-in-law and her three children, 1976.

KNIGHTS OF THE SUN

Joseph Di Mambro was born in France in 1925 but moved to Quebec, in the French-speaking region of Canada. He made money in the jewellery trade before moving back to Europe and investing in real estate. At the height of his affluence, he was said to have owned about 60 properties around the world.

In 1972, he was indicted and found guilty on charges of fraud. In 1974, he founded a spiritual organization, The Centre of Study in the New Age, based first at Annemasse in Switzerland and then at Collonges-sous-Saleve in France. The latter centre, known as The Pyramid, burnt down under doubtful circumstances in 1979. Di Mambro then moved to Geneva and established another organization, which was known as the Golden Way and was named after the nineteenth-century English order of occult hermeticists, Golden Dawn. From 1982, this organization became grouped into cells of initiates and adepts known as Club Amenta. It was at Annemasse that Di Mambro joined forces with Luc Jouret, although Di Mambro was always considered to be the business brain behind the partnership that founded and ran the Temple du Soleil. Di Mambro was married twice and his second spouse, a Québécoise, born Jocelyne Duplessis, bore him a daughter, Emmanuelle. Di Mambro also had a son, Elie, by his first marriage. The entire family perished, along with Luc Jouret, at Granges-sur-Salvan.

Luc Jouret was born in the Belgian Congo in 1947 and served as a paratrooper in Zaire, where he learned, among other skills, the technique of manufacturing delayed-action fire bombs. He went on to qualify as a doctor of medicine but became increasingly interested in unorthodox therapies. He turned to homeopathic and alternative medicine, opening a clinic in 1978 at Annemasse, where he was under the influence of Joseph Di Mambro. By this time he had travelled the world extensively and, in so doing, developed a fascination with eastern mysticism. Some of his time had been spent in India studying with a guru. When he reached Annemasse he joined Di Mambro's solar and magic cult, the Golden Way.

Jouret cultivated a charismatic oratory style and from the early 1980s was giving talks on solar mysticism at Di Mambro's cult centres – Club Amenata in Switzerland and a spread of similar cells, known as Club Archedia, in Canada. All of the cult centres were run by Di Mambro's wife, Jocelyne.

THE NEW KNIGHTS TEMPLAR

In 1984, with Joseph Di Mambro, Jouret founded a highly secretive sect known as OICTS (*Ordre International Chevaleresque Tradition Solaire*), which he claimed was descended from the charter of the medieval Knights Templar and from which evolved the cult known popularly as Le Temple du Soleil – in English, the Temple of the Sun. His lectures from the Club Amenta days were subsequently sold on cassette and his articles also appeared regularly in a cult journal called *Excalibur*.

Within the Temple du Soleil he was the undisputed guru. It was his preoccupation with the forthcoming apocalypse and the belief that he and his followers could be saved by fire that set him on a course toward emulating the fate of the Templars – most of whom were burnt at the stake for heresy (see pages 42–3). Jouret was obsessed with the idea of regeneration through fire and with the significance of 21/22 December, which is the period of the Winter Solstice, the time of the year when the Sun is at its weakest angle in the northern hemisphere. With this in mind, he persuaded his followers that he was actually a time-traveller, who possessed the powers to lead them to a distant galaxy, where they would undergo a spiritual and physical rebirth.

Jouret was originally thought to have escaped the mass suicides that took place in Switzerland on the night of 4 October 1994. However, his charred corpse was later identified from dental records. He had perished in one of the two main locations of the cult, at Granges-sur-Salvan.

There emerged, subsequently, indications that Jouret had first contemplated a similar fate in Canada in the spring of 1993, but that the plan had to be postponed after he was arrested for flouting Canadian gun laws.

THE MASS SUICIDE

It was said that Joseph Di Mambro's 12-year-old daughter, Emanuelle, had provided the innocent catalyst for the holocaust that followed. Di Mambro claimed that she was the product of divine conception and was spiritually unique. He thus violently objected when a boy born to Canadian cult members Antonio Dutoit and his wife was subsequently named Emmanuel. The boy was, he argued, the incarnation of the Antichrist and therefore had to be destroyed. This in fact led to the slaughter of the family and started the momentum toward mass suicide when

it became clear that the police were linking the murders to the Temple of the Sun.

Joseph Di Mambro and Luc Jouret were, however, also under investigation on suspicion of illegal arms dealing and money laundering on a sizeable scale. The net was, in any event, closing on them.

Above: Joseph Di Mambro with his wife Jocelyne and daughter Emmanuelle, who he claimed was the next Messiah.

MESSIAH OF THE LONELY HEARTS

Born in 1920, this North Korean preacher claims a worldwide following of between two and three million devotees and once earned a place in *The Guinness Book of Records* for having staged a mass wedding of 30,000 couples in the Olympic Stadium in Seoul, in 1992.

At a similar satellite- and Internet-managed spectacular in 2000, he eclipsed this with the marriage of 450,000 couples. At birth, Sun Myung Moon, which means Shining Sun and Moon, was given the name Young Myung Moon, a slightly less glamorous title meaning merely Shining Dragon Moon. At the age of 10, Moon was converted from Buddhism to Christianity, when his parents joined a Presbyterian church. Six years later, on Easter Monday, he claims to have received a message from Christ requesting that he continue the work that He had been unable to complete some 2,000 years earlier. He rapidly came to regard himself as the embodiment of the Second Coming of the Messiah, whose responsibility it was to control the world by whatever means lay at his disposal. These means, inevitably, relied on a liberal supply of funds and his disciples were encouraged to raise it from the public at large.

In his earlier years, spurred on by the revelations he had received as a 16-year-old, Moon developed his own version of the Bible entitled *Divine Principle*, before emigrating to Japan, where he graduated in electrical engineering. He returned to Korea at the end of World War Two and, at the age of 34, founded the Unification Church (more recently identified by the title of the Family Federation for World Peace and Unification). Arrested in 1948 on charges of inciting social disorder, Moon was liberated by the Americans, whereupon, legend has it, he cycled 600 miles to Pusan in South Korea with a fellow ex-prisoner on his back. In 1955, he was imprisoned again, albeit briefly.

He married three times, but the first two unions ended in divorce, though gave him a son by his first wife. His third marriage was to Hak Ja Han, said to translate as 'True Mother', who bore him a family of 14 children. During the 1960s, Moon campaigned against Communism in Korea and developed a deep and lasting hatred for its philosophies – he has always argued that the converse of Communism is Theism. Perhaps understandably, he gravitated toward the USA, the home of Capitalism. He travelled extensively in the USA, where a small cell of the Unification Church had already been pioneered by Korean ex-patriots during 1959. By 1972, again on specific instructions from God, he had purchased his first Unification Church property in New York State and elected to settle in the USA. In the years between 1975 and 1985, the Unification Church headquarters received substantial sums of money from the worldwide movement.

When, in 1984, he found himself fined $25,000 and taken back to prison for 18 months on charges of tax evasion, a $5 million public relations exercise was mounted on his behalf with the intention of making him appear as a religious martyr. Moon turned his attention to the People's Republic of China during the late 1980s. He also achieved a meeting with Mikhail Gorbachev in 1990, when he was given the go-ahead to send his missionaries to Russia. More recently, he provided financial backing for the French Politician Jean Marie Le Pen's right-wing election campaign in France.

MOON THE MARRIAGE BROKER

Curiously, for one with such evangelical zeal, Moon never mastered the English language and, in the USA, delivered his lengthy orations, given several times a week and often lasting for several hours, through translators in his native Korean tongue. Those who witnessed his performances testify, nevertheless, to his compelling personality and zeal. He is said to have bounced around the platform with great energy, hectoring and lambasting those who follow the Satanic path, which effectively encompasses the rest of humanity outside of the Moon organization. He proclaimed that he and his wife were the true heavenly parents of all followers but his most notorious innovation was to use his own exclusive judgement to select marriage partners for his flock. Often these were couples who had never met and who frequently did not even speak the same language. It was in this context that he presided over the vast assemblies of brides and grooms whose pledge to each other frequently resulted *de facto* in a lifetime of spiritual and financial devotion to the Reverend Moon.

In 2009, Moon passed the reins of his church to his youngest son, the Revd Hyung Jin Moon. Sun Myung Moon died on 3 September 2012, aged 92.

Opposite: Sun Myung Moon and his wife bless over 3,000 newlyweds, South Korea, 2002.

WARREN STEED JEFFS

In the latest roll call of religious movers and shakers, few can claim the dubious accolade of having been on the FBI's "Ten Most Wanted List".

One such icon in the shadowy world of the fringe cults is Warren Steed Jeffs, arrested on the Interstate 15 highway near Las Vegas in Nevada on 6 May 2006, and arraigned on charges of having sex with a minor, conspiracy to have sex with a minor, accomplice to rape and unlawful flight to avoid prosecution.

Warren Jeffs is the President of the tortuously named Fundamentalist Church of Jesus Christ of Latter Day Saints, more conveniently referred to as the FLDS. He is also, according to his followers, a prophet and seer, and revelatory of God's will on behalf of humanity. That Jeffs can be described as saintly is, however, unlikely. Born on 3 December 1955, he and his father, Rulon T. Jeffs, moved into Colorado City, a town on the Arizona-Utah border, in 1998, and began to preach of an impending apocalypse with Salt Lake City in the eye of the heavenly storm. In a familiar message that has been trotted out by numerous religious despots throughout the history of cults, Rulon and Warren proclaimed that only true believers, pure and perfect in following the teachings of the sect, would be saved.

Warren Jeffs is described as a tall, lanky individual with the mesmerixing manner and powers of oratory that have so often characterized successful cult leaders. He assumed leadership of the FLDS in May 2005, taking on the mantle of his father, who died in September 2003 at the age of 92. Rulon T. Jeffs left behind a trust worth in the region of $100 million, most of the real estate of Colorado City and neighbouring Hildale, a city borough that lies just across the Arizona state line in Utah, an estimated 75 grieving widows and 65 children.

Colorado City is a remote and secluded place, hemmed in by mountains, which makes it an ideal location to exert ideological control, and the members of the sect appear to live in something of a timewarp, with the modern world kept largely at bay. Children are schooled at home, so that in a community of about 7,000 residents only some 100 attend the single public school. Laughter causes the spirit of God to leak from the body, so is frowned upon; dating and courtship are not allowed. Women are wholly subservient, wear demure ankle-length dresses, buttoned-up, high-necked blouses and affect hairstyles from a past era. Swimming is taboo since it would require girls to appear in swimsuits. According to one of the sect's former members, Flora Jessop, who fled the sect in 1986 after being forced to marry a cousin, Warren Jeffs "decides who marries whom and when", often at little more than a few hours' notice. Under a regime reminiscent of the Taliban in Afghanistan, FLDS women are treated as second-class citizens to the extent that, in his pulpit rhetoric, Jeffs has asserted that they may only enter heaven at the behest of their husbands. Yet few break free of the cloak of intimidation in a society where obedience is paramount, where to err is to risk eternal damnation and where God is allegedly ready to punish through the iron hand of His prophet on earth.

In history, the FLDS took over where the Mormon Church left off in the nineteenth century, when it denounced polygamy under pressure from the US government. The fundamentalists broke away from the mother church and continue to practise the form of plural marriage that the Mormon founder, Brigham Young, had espoused. They believe that Warren Jeffs, as commander-in-chief, was, or is, in direct communication with God, who apparently advised him and his father that polygamy is desirable. In FLDS thinking, in order to reach the highest echelons of a hereafter polygamist heaven, a man must have gained at least three wives and the prophet has decreed that Jeffs is the only member of the sect who can perform marriage ceremonies and assign wives to husbands. Gaining the approval of Warren

FBI TEN MOST WANTED FUGITIVE

UNLAWFUL FLIGHT TO AVOID PROSECUTION - SEXUAL CONDUCT WITH A MINOR, CONSPIRACY TO COMMIT SEXUAL CONDUCT WITH A MINOR; RAPE AS AN ACCOMPLICE

WARREN STEED JEFFS

Jeffs is therefore the route to acquiring more females, a route that involves compliance, ready servitude and the handing over of salary cheques. Conversely, a man who loses the favours of the prophet can find his wives being removed from his household and reassigned. Warren Jeffs has assured his place in eternity by allegedly acquiring between 50 and 70 spouses, including most of his father's widows, although the exact number is unclear.

Much of the sect's assets, including real estate owned by an FLDS Trust and controlled by Warren Jeffs, were under the administration of the Utah courts, pending litigation, but before his arrest his authority was fairly omnipotent. The sect owned virtually all the property in which its members reside and default or failure to abide by the rules could result in forcible eviction. In common with many fundamentalist sectarian leaders, Warren Jeffs also enforced the segregation of FLDS families from the rest of society and placed an embargo on news. At one stage a bevy of his lieutenants, known as the God Squad,

Above: Jeffs's appearance in the FBI's Most Wanted handout.

was authorized to search homes in order to establish that they contained only approved literature.

The authorities began to close in on Jeffs in the summer of 2005 when charges were issued following his alleged supervision of marriage between a 16-year-old girl and a 28-year-old policeman, a sect member who was already married. Wanted posters appeared indicting a $10,000 reward for information leading to Jeffs' capture. By May 2006, he was on the "Ten Most Wanted List" of the FBI, when it was also claimed that he had been defrauding the FLDS Trust Fund of assets. The price on his head had also gone up to $100,000 and dire warnings were issued that he was possibly travelling with armed bodyguards. Following his arrest, little is known about who, if anybody, has taken control of the Colorado City sect in his absence.

MILLENNIUM

Now that we have passed the year 2000, a critical date in the diaries of so many cult followers during the 1990s, emphasis has shifted. Christianity, still heading on a downward path, with attendances falling at churches throughout the northern hemisphere, is fighting back with an increasing focus on "modernization" and with greater reliance on sectarian informality, trendy songs and "happy clapping" to replace more traditional services. The threat of Armageddon through nuclear war with the former Soviet block is now passé and, since the horror of 9/11, "Bible Belt" America probably sees the threat of Islamic expansion and militancy as its greatest challenge.

The cult movements of the 1990s that too often wound themselves up into the hysteria of mass suicides and other tragedies have lost much of their impetus and allure. Some have refocused on global warming, excessive materialism, and indeed the growing conflict with more radical Islam as evidence that the end of the world is still nigh, but their activities are no longer especially newsworthy in the face of more dramatic events. Gestures of suicide to escape an impending holocaust have been replaced by similar gestures in the name of Allah and of what is seen as a need to reject growing Western influence on Islamic society. An essential difference lies in the fact that Islamic extremists are not content to make lone gestures but favour taking large sections of the population along with them. In this final section, we examine the downward slide of some of the more radical sects that once bathed in pre-millennium popularity and take an objective look at those that have emerged since the year 2000.

THE RETURN OF AUM

Shoko Asahara was committed for trial in the spring of 1996; the court proceedings lasted for eight years until February 2004, when he was found guilty and sentenced to death, the Japanese Supreme Court having rejected his final appeal in September 2006.

Cases against cult members were expected to be wound up by the end of 1999, but this does not seem to have taken into account the extremely pedestrian pace of the Japanese legal system, which does not always deal with cases over a consecutive period of days. Asahara was led back and forth into Criminal Court Room 104 of the Tokyo District Court over an extraordinary length of time to hear the drawn out defence and prosecution arguments in his case. He persistently pleaded "Not guilty" to the 17 charges against him, including most notably the Sarin gas attacks on the Tokyo underground and in Matsumota, and throughout he remained unrepentant about his religious aims.

In 1997, Japan's Public Security Commission reached what, in hindsight, is viewed as a dangerously flawed decision. On the grounds that Aum had become too ineffectual to pose a danger to society, the Commission turned down demands to ban the cult. This decision was arrived at partly on the consideration that, in 1996, the cult had been liquidated as a commercial enterprise and its assets seized. Today, however, Aum Shinri Kyo is said to have largely rebuilt its financial power base through some astute dealings. Its position has been assisted by the general economic slump in Japan, which has frequently resulted in commercial enterprises coming on to the market for auction at knock-down prices. Aum is believed to be the controlling hand behind a chain of retail computer stores which amassed profits of over $61 million in 1998. Shop workers shrugged off the claims of Aum ownership as idle rumour. With the revenue earned the cult was said to be buying up other properties and recruiting new members. Since February 1999, Aum has allegedly purchased at least five fairly substantial properties, including factory sites around Tokyo. Because many of these acquisitions came through agents or dummy corporations, however, the tracing of actual ownership becomes extremely difficult and there is no concrete evidence that Aum is linked to any or all of them.

After Asahara's detention in 1995, the leadership of Aum Shinri Kyo was temporarily taken over by a former spokesperson of the cult, Fumihiro Joyu, who was then imprisoned also. The cult's administration is currently run by one of Asahara's daughters, Rika Matsumoto. The public face of the organization is masterminded by a graduate school dropout, Hiroshi Araki, whose team operates from a commercial building identified ostensibly as Sato Engineering in Tokyo's Yanaka district. Predictably, Araki is quick to play down Aum's expansion programme, arguing that the claims made against it are widely exaggerated. He insists that the cult's finances remain at subsistence level and that Aum owns no properties. He also dispenses reassuring figures suggesting that the membership of the cult has dropped from about 12,000 before the Tokyo subway outrage to a mere 1,000.

Japanese officialdom now views the position differently, however, and concern is mounting that Aum may be about to pose a renewed threat, not merely in Japan but elsewhere in the world. The Public Security authorities believe that Aum owns at least 30 "facilities" and some 100 residential compounds, housing up to 2,000 members. These potential commune sites probably concern the authorities most since what takes place on privately owned territory cannot be dictated or controlled by Japanese law and they thus represent free breeding ground for insurrection.

In May 1999, a company called Arefu reserved a hall at the Performing Arts Centre in Nagoya City for a concert, which is claimed to have been little more than a recruiting seminar by Aum Shinri Kyo. Arefu operates from the same address as the cult's Nagoya office, and it has been suggested that most of the "concert-goers" were current or new members of the cult. An increasing number of residential communities are also reporting worries about the activities of Aum. Inhabitants of a village close by one of the properties said to be owned by the cult have been so concerned about the conduct of their neighbours that they have installed CCTV cameras and excavated a deep trench around the village boundary in order to keep Aum members away.

To no small extent the momentum of what is still arguably Japan's most dangerous cult was kept going during Asahara's incarceration through warnings issued from his prison cell about an Armageddon scenario that was to take place in September 1999, in which all but Aum members would be vaporized. His messages lost credibility when this did not happen.

More recently, on the other hand, there have been concerns about the position of the new leader of the Aum Shinri Kyo, Fumihiro Joyu. He was released from prison on 29 December 1999, and was expected to renew Asahara's uncompromisingly dangerous message. Joyu, however, pledged the cult to a more peaceful line and encouraged an atmosphere of conciliation with the Japanese public and authorities. Under his leadership, Aum Shinri Kyo changed its name to Aleph, the first letter of the Hebrew alphabet. There can, however, be no complacency. There are reports, according to the Japanese equivalent of the FBI, that since 2005, Aum has been split politically into two factions, one of which includes those hard-line members of the cult still pledged to keeping faith with Ashara's more extreme and militant legacy, which amounts to justifying murder to achieve its ends.

DO AND TI — PEDDLERS OF DOOM

One of the most bizarre unions in the history of cult movements was that forged almost 30 years ago in the 1970s between Marshall Applewhite, an inmate of a US mental hospital, and one of his nurses named Bonnie Nettles.

Applewhite had become convinced that he was sent to Earth as a witness on behalf of a superior heavenly power known as the "Older Member in the Evolutionary Level above Human". He persuaded Nettles of his exclusive mission and she became both his spiritual acolyte and temporal partner until her death from cancer in 1985. The pair founded the Heaven's Gate movement in 1977 and took on the spiritual titles of Do and Ti while also referring to themselves, for the benefit of their students, as Bo and Peep. The analogy which they set out to convey was one of shepherds searching out lost sheep and guiding them to safety through the gateway of heaven. Cult members became organized under the tutelage of Applewhite and Nettles much in the style of students working to complete an academic course. Into the more tried and tested aspects of the course training was introduced a "high tech" element in the shape of an intergalactic spacecraft travelling toward Earth in the tail of the Hale-Bopp comet.

According to the Heaven's Gate doctrine that Applewhite promoted, time spent on earth was a training period and Hale-Bopp was the long-awaited "marker" for graduation, after which the disembodied souls of cult recruits would be beamed up, *Star Trek*-fashion to the waiting craft. There was, in the view of Heaven's Gate devotees, a downside to remaining on Earth since they believe that it is due to be "recycled" and the only chance of survival is, needless to say, to join the extraterrestrial exodus.

It has been claimed that the cult started in Montana but, unlike many others, it seems never to have benefited from a fixed address and instead its virtual reality home has been the Internet. Before the mass suicide of its members, they were constantly moving from one rented address to another, largely circulating through Arizona and New Mexico. Much of the information which the press gleaned about Heaven's Gate came from an ex-member, a computer designer named Richard Ford,

who took the cult name Rio d'Angelo and who left the group four weeks before the bizarre events which catapulted it into the limelight at Rancho Santa Fe.

As early as 1975, the preachings of Do and Ti were the subject of considerable derision in America as the promises they made became increasingly bizarre and self-adulatory, including the claim that they would shortly hold a press conference with the President of the United States on the White House lawn concerning the imminent apocalypse. The couple firmly believed that they were the "witnesses" described in chapter 11 of the Biblical Book of Revelation: "And I will give power unto my two witnesses, and they shall prophecy a thousand two hundred and threescore days, clothed in sackcloth." [Rev. 11:3]

Under the weight of public antagonism, the cult effectively went underground in 1976, re-emerging, with advertisements placed in newspapers across America to announce their presence, first in 1988 and then again in 1993. On this last occasion they hinted, ominously, that the only effective means of entering the spacecraft and travelling to the Heaven's Gate was by terminating their lives. They seem, in spite of claims which many would regard as the ramblings of deranged minds, to have been successful in recruiting cult members from various walks of life, including an accountable number of intellectuals.

The paranoia of Applewhite and Nettles toward civil authority, and the extent of Applewhite's mental derangement, became increasingly apparent. Following the death of his partner, and convinced that alien presences were plotting against the cult, he arranged for Heaven's Gate to take out an insurance policy in October 1996 at an annual premium of £1,000, under which each member stood to receive about $1 million in the event of abduction, impregnation or death under alien attack.

Referring to each other as "brother" and "sister", members were encouraged by Applewhite to create a

Left: A young and wholesome-looking Marshall Applewhite.

monkish appearance wearing black pyjama suits and the organization took on a generally monastic tone. To the outside world, at the time of the mass suicide of members in 1998, Applewhite was being described as a tall older man, extremely pale, and known as "Brother John".

Applewhite claimed that, after the death of Nettles, he remained in direct spiritual contact with her and that Ti was travelling aboard the space craft under the direct guidance of the Older Member and in command of the rescue mission. Applewhite himself perished in the suicide pact.

CHEN TAO – GOD'S SALVATION CHURCH

Among the most recently formed of the so-called "doomsday cults", Chen Tao, meaning "True Way", is considered by observers in the USA to be particularly dangerous, with its leadership once suspected of contemplating a mass suicide bid.

The cult was founded in 1996 by a 42-year-old Taiwanese national, Hon Ming Chen, a one-time lecturer at the Chianan College of Pharmacology and Science who claims to have received his spiritual guidance from Yu Hsia Chen. The cult moved into the USA in 1997 and became established briefly in San Dimas, California, under the title God's Salvation Church. Shortly afterward, Chen purchased a property in the town of Garland, Texas, claiming that the name sounded like "God's Land". In a tragic irony, the purchase was completed on 26 March 1997, the day before the Heaven's Gate mass suicide at Rancho Santa Fe.

Within a short space of time, some 150 cult members were buying properties in the neighbourhood and became a familiar sight dressed in Chinese "coolie" hats and white tunics and riding around on bicycles, an exercise allegedly designed to prepare for the arrival of God's Kingdom in America.

During the summer of 1997 Chen broadcast that he had located the reincarnation of Jesus Christ in the shape of a resident of Vancouver in Canada, although this contender for the messianic role was ousted in favour of a nine-year-old child, Che-Yu Chiang. Chen had already located the next Buddha in a small boy, Chi Jen Lo, aged 10, and his professed intention was to see the two incarnate leaders of the great religions come together for a meeting.

Chen also announced the startling news that God in person would appear on worldwide TV on 25 March 1998 at 12.01 a.m. US Central Standard Time before descending to earth on 31 March. When the TV broadcast did not take place, Chen felt obliged to warn that the even more momentous event scheduled for six days later was unlikely to occur. God, it was claimed, had not let the faithful down, however, because he had actually appeared as promised in the collective guise of members of the Chen Tao cult.

In May 1998, the cult headquarters at Garland was largely abandoned, many of the members returning to Taiwan with expired visas and the remainder moving north first, to Olcott in New York State, and then to Lockport, a little way south of Niagara Falls.

Chen Tao philosophy appears to constitute a confusing mix of Christianity, Buddhism, local Taiwanese folk religion and belief in heaven-sent UFOs. Chen described beings, both good and bad, created in a "central vortex" before passing into the material realm. In a book published in 1996 he elaborates on the existence of three souls – the physical soul, the main spiritual light, of which the average human being possesses about three million degrees, and the conscious soul – all of which become dispersed at death. Ranged against the good beings are entities known as "outside spirits" which, interestingly, control virtually all other Taiwanese Buddhist religious movements. Strongly anti-Communist in tone, the Chen Tao doctrine argues that the earth has suffered a series of apocalyptic upheavals, each of which has culminated in nuclear war. In each case limited numbers of the faithful have been airlifted to safety in flying saucers before being deposited back on Earth, where they have lived underground until the radiation levels have dropped sufficiently. Chen proclaimed that the area of the Great Lakes was likely to be the most favoured place of ultimate refuge, one of the factors influencing his decision to emigrate from Taiwan to North America.

The next in line end-of-world scenario was scheduled for 1999. It was anticipated that there would be a military blockade of Taiwan by mainland China linked with an economic collapse of the "Tiger economies" and resulting in mass starvation. North and South Korea were also predicted to unite and Japan to undergo militaristic expansion. This combined tumult was to result in nuclear holocaust and, in order to avoid the final chapter, Chen

Tao was primed for a mass suicide on 31 March 1999. Nothing untoward took place and the next date of doomsday was set a little later in the year, sometime between 1 October and 31 December 1999. The world again kept turning. In the years since, membership has dwindled and it is uncertain if any faction of Chen Tao still exists. Hon Ming Chen's whereabouts are also unknown and hasn't been heard from in many years.

Above: A family returning to their home after God did not appear on television in 1998 as planned. The cowboy hats were part of the church's dress code.

CONCERNED CHRISTIANS

Although few of the cults to have emerged within the second half of the twentieth century were specifically focused on the millennium in the sense of the thousand-year period marking a Second Coming or the dawn of a New Age, several of the "doomsday" organizations anticipated the much-vaunted apocalypse taking place at around the time of the millennium.

Among those fringe religious organizations that achieved a degree of notoriety linked with the apocalyptic scenario is the Denver-based cult known as the "Concerned Christians". Founded in Colorado by Monte Kim Miller in the early 1980s, it was established as an activist group with the mandate of fighting a perceived threat to Christianity in North America posed by the New Age movement. It then

adopted an increasingly apocalyptic view linked with belief that the Second Coming was imminent and developed a paranoia toward authority or jurisdiction emanating from any other quarter than its own.

In common with many cult leaders, Miller steadily became convinced of his own messianic vocation and, in June 1996, announced that he "spoke for God", a proclamation which caused sufficient concern among some of his followers that they chose to break ranks and abandon the organization.

The following year, Miller predicted, on behalf of Concerned Christians, that the onset of the millennium apocalypse would take the form of a massive earthquake, which was to strike the city of Denver on 10 October 1998. Shortly afterward, according to the *Denver Post*, the 44-year-old Miller and his wife, Marcie, filed for bankruptcy and then faded from view in company with a group of somewhere between 50 and 70 cult followers. A number of them had sold their homes and possessions and the intention appears to have been to escape the impending disaster of which Miller had warned.

The destination of at least some members of the group was the Middle East since Miller claimed that his destiny was to die violently in Jerusalem in 1999 during December and to be resurrected three days later. Toward the end of October 1998, the FBI authorities in the USA passed a precautionary warning to counterparts in Israel since concern was mounting that cult members were planning to provoke a violent incident on the streets of Jerusalem in order to facilitate Miller's self-proclaimed fate. During the following month, 10 or more cult members were identified as having arrived in Jerusalem though Miller was apparently not among them.

Concerned Christians came to occupy the headlines of the international press on 5 January 1999 in the aftermath of a police raid on two houses in the Jerusalem suburb of Mevasseret Zion during the previous Sunday. These properties had been rented allegedly by members of the cult and three of the people living there were taken in for questioning though later released. In total, 14 cult members including six children, all travelling on United States passports, were deported to Denver on the following Saturday despite requests by some to be allowed to join fellow Concerned Christian devotees in Greece. Miller, according to cult members, was in London at the time of the raid but the Israeli police investigation revolved around a possible conspiracy to bomb holy places. An Israeli security official contended that the Concerned Christians were preparing for a "big provocation" on the Temple Mount aimed at instigating a war between Arabs and Jews that would culminate in Armageddon.

The concern of the Israeli authorities had been heightened by a press reporter's discovery, on the Monday evening, of a taped message left on the doorstep of one of the rented houses. The voice of the narrator has not been identified but a researcher based at the Center for Millennial Studies in the University of Boston has claimed that the voice and style of preaching resembles that on other tapes issued by Miller.

The message includes a doomsday warning the implications of which were taken up at the time of the Israeli incident in one of the most respected United States newspapers focusing on religious issues, *The Salt Lake Tribune*. Press commentator Elaine Ruth Fletcher expressed concern at the title of the tape, which was found to be dated as early as 25 June 1997. The heading "I am the Lawmaker" and some of the content were reminiscent of the cant which had been adopted in the 1960s by Charles Manson, the infamous cult leader at the centre of the Sharon Tate slayings. Manson had also frequently used the "Lawmaker" phrase and it is said that his name crops up several times during the taped message. On the tape, Manson apparently equates his life and purpose with those of Jesus Christ. The message also includes references to the Second Coming of Christ coupled with allegations that the USA is a "dragon kingdom", which will earn retribution considerably more severe than that delivered upon Japan at the end of World War II.

Arab–Israeli war did indeed break out, but not as a result of any provocation by sectarians on the Temple Mount. Today, little is known of the cult as it functioned prior to the millennium. For a time, members are believed to have continued with a level of activity in Greece before being thrown out. Today, one can discover an Internet site entitled "Concerned Christians". It, however, advises visitors that it is a non-profit organization aiming its evangelism specifically at the Mormon community "to educate them about the deception of Mormonism and to equip them for service with the truth of God's Word, the Holy Bible". Membership is said to include Christians and former Mormons who have "come to know Jesus as the Lord and Saviour of their lives". Whether this Concerned Christian organization has any links with that of the same name formerly run by Monte Kim Miller is unclear.

Opposite: Cult member John Bayles being led to a court hearing by Israeli police.

JESUS ARMY AND FELLOWSHIP CHURCH

In its promotional literature, Jesus Army claims to be neither a cult nor a new religious group but rather the "gospel and social outreach identity of the Jesus Fellowship Church", stated to be an independent evangelical Christian organization with a congregation of about 2,500, many of whom live communally in a sub-organization referred to as the New Creation Christian Community.

Though arguably launched in about 1969, most of the founder members did not come together into communal retreats until 1974 when they began to sell their homes and pool resources to buy larger properties.

Currently, the headquarters of Jesus Army is based in a farmhouse at Nether Heyford in Northampton, England, and, like several other modern religious movements, it carries out much of its evangelism on the Internet, where devotees are depicted in scenes of joy, love and utopian togetherness. The leader and self-styled "Senior Pastor" is Noel Stanton. Said to be a highly persuasive man about whom, in 1997, the Northampton South MP Michael Morris urged potential recruits to be "very careful", Stanton appears in his website pictures as a benevolent grey-haired individual with a chubby smile and a charismatic manner.

The organization runs regular Sunday-evening events at Spinney Hill Hall in Northampton. The meetings, endearingly titled Heart, offer admittance free of charge and a warm welcome is extended to all. These meetings, the website information stresses, are the "mould-breaking events that everyone's talking about – relaxed and powerful". The rhetoric goes on, "Have a taste, you'll be hooked! Everyone's welcome, everyone's loved".

In order to advance its aims of recruitment, Jesus Army runs regular training programmes. Within the ideology of the organization much value is placed on "personal mentoring", a significant aspect whereby disciples "help to reach the spiritually hungry people of the UK and build the living church of Jesus while enjoying a shared lifestyle of simplicity and sacrifice". In reality, "simplicity and sacrifice" means that members

Right: Members of the Jesus Army show their togetherness at a group meeting.

are required to pool their goods, income, resources and abilities. This handing-over of material assets is required from the outset and is even mandatory for those embarking on a two-year probationary period before becoming full community members. This, in the attractive language of the sect, is "a breakthrough into the challenge of living as shared lifestyle".

Much of the Jesus Army recruitment seems to be carried on through what is described as "night time evangelism and outreach" in London's West End. Many members are said to be drawn from the inner cities, where Jesus Army concentrates on young homeless people, taking them into some 100 large community houses, which have been bought up by the sect around the country. The Army claims that it actually attracts a wide range of converts, from intellectuals to drug addicts and village chapel-goers to hippies.

Current estimates from within the organization are that some 600 members live communally in about 60 centres known as "New Creation Christian Communities", while the rest, an estimated 1,800, retain their own homes. Toward the end of the 1990s, the Church was named as an umbrella for several commercial organizations, including a health food wholesale business called House of Goodness, employing about 90 members; a construction firm known as Towcaster Building Supplies; and Skano Services, a company involved in road haulage operations. The House of Goodness advertises on the web but Skano Services apparently no longer functions. There also exists a Towcester Building Supplies company, but there is no current indication of any links, commercial or otherwise, between this company and Jesus Army.

In April 1997, however, the *News of the World* published an article exposing a less attractive side to the cult's "challenge of living as shared lifestyle". Posing as a down-and-out, one of the newspaper's investigative journalists stayed briefly at the Nether Heyford headquarters. According to his subsequent report, some 100 devotees were living at the farm, styling themselves as "brothers" and "sisters", sharing their property communally and living a celibate life in separate quarters. When not working or taking meals, members were regularly involved in prayer and in analysing their sinful pasts before having found the redemption of Jesus Army. The requirement to give up possessions included, the journalist discovered, all earnings and even unemployment giro cheques.

The *News of the World* investigation resulted from a court case involving a teenage female disciple, Eirene Clarke, and an elder of the cult, Edwin Jindu, who was found guilty at Isleworth Crown Court on two out of three counts of indecent assault. The 18-year-old victim – whose parents had been members of the Jesus Fellowship Church and who had lived in the sect since birth – claimed that the organization "deprived me of a childhood, robbed me of my innocence, ruined my life … and I thought it was in the name of God". Clarke alleged that, over a two-year period after she had reached the age of 13, Jindu subjected her to an ordeal of repeated sexual assault at Nether Heyford, where women were seen as second-class citizens, required to cook and clean up after the men.

Other disillusioned cult members also signed sworn testimonies for the *News of the World*, claiming abuse within the Jesus Army. The Fellowship claims that members who wish to withdraw from the community are eligible for refund of their capital contribution and that almost all "remain in warm contact with friends in the Fellowship". Reminiscent of the policies of many comparable organizations, however, ex-members who decided to leave, or were obliged to terminate their association with the community, having formed relationships with non-cult members, claim to have been warned that, in so doing, they were heading for eternal damnation.

The cult has not been the subject of further adverse publicity and in 2001, in a desire to promote a healthy and positive image, one of its houses was opened to the media. A Channel 4 TV documentary entitled "Battlecentre" followed the activities of a section of the commune operating from a large house (the Battlcentre) in a rundown London suburb. It claimed to open its doors to all, including muggers, drug dealers and murderers, who then lived alongside families, graduates and pensioners. Inmates pledged to start a new life and accept Jesus as saviour. The house is currently owned by the Jesus Army and is said to be managed by an ex-acid dropping hippie.

HEAVEN'S GATE

Undoubtedly the most notorious among the recent spate of space-orientated religious movements has been the US-based cult known as Heaven's Gate. Founded in Montana in 1977 by Marshall Applewhite, its members claim to be guided by the "Older Member in the Evolutionary Level above Human" and his (or her) earthly representative.

The realm of the Older Member is a heavenly place to which cult devotees will be transported by a spacecraft sent from the Evolutionary Level and accessed through the "Gate".

As the first offspring of the Older Member, Jesus Christ features strongly in Heaven's Gate ideology. Two thousand years ago, according to cult teaching, a member of the Kingdom was motivated to move into a human body in order to offer a way leading to membership of the Kingdom of Heaven. Cult ideology believes that by that time in history civilization had progressed sufficiently for

bodies to be used as "soul containers" but that some 2,000 years were to elapse before another "guide" was born. Until the much-reported mass suicide of cult members, Christ's modern counterpart was referred to as Do, a spiritual name which is seemingly a corruption of the expression "John Doe" meaning, in American police jargon, an unidentified body. This self-styled messianic figure, in reality an inmate of a Montana mental institution, Marshall Applewhite had access to more effective communication facilities than those afforded to Jesus at the time of the Sermon on the

Mount. He saw strong advantage in disseminating his gospel through the Internet.

The cult demanded familiar impositions of isolation from the rest of society, claiming the need to "leave the world behind", including family, sensuality and selfish desire. Members were allegedly celibate. Of greater concern, they were taught the necessity to abandon the human mind and if necessary, the human body, a feature of most of the suicide-inclined cults. The principles seem, however, to have combined bits of gnosticism with a sort of techno-religion. Heaven's Gate followers believed that after the dissolution of their human frames, they would lie as corpses for three days before being raised from the dead into their awaiting spaceship, which was circling the earth conveniently disguised as a cloud.

They are, in effect, religious UFO watchers with a strong sense of paranoia toward the rest of society. According to the information Heaven's Gate broadcast on the Internet, its enemies are those who maintain the norms of today's civilized world. Once students of the Kingdom, these oppressors of the truth dropped out of the classroom and are to be viewed as fallen angels referred to as space aliens or Luciferans. Disguised in establishment clothing, they use discarnate spirits, or minds disembodied at the point of death, to achieve their purpose against members of the cult by programming the rest of society to accept straitjacketed beliefs according to what is socially and politically correct. The argument proceeds that these "space aliens in business suits" do not wish to be found out and therefore condemn any exploration of radical religious concepts. Psychologists would argue that this is typical persecution mania.

Although devotees believed that they had an escape route from cataclysmic events surrounding the end of the century, Heaven's Gate was not so much a millennium cult as one whose destiny was, members claimed, linked to the appearance of the comet Hale-Bopp, in the shadow of which a rescue spaceship travelled toward Earth. It has also turned out to be a suicide cult in the

dramatic fashion of the Jonestown Peoples' Temple and the more recent Temple du Soleil.

On 27 March 1997, 39 cult members elected to speed their passage through Heaven's Gate in a mass suicide. It was ex-member Rio d'Angelo who allegedly found the bodies after receiving a tip-off video from the cult; he then alerted the San Diego police to the deaths. This bizarre culmination, which involved 21 women and 18 men, took place in a rented $10,000-a-month villa in the exclusive Californian neighbourhood of Rancho Santa Fe, just outside the city limits of Santa Fe. For the previous six months, Heaven's Gate members living there had maintained a low profile, apparently running a commercial enterprise known as the Higher Source and providing computer programming for Californian businesses requiring web pages on the Internet. The operation promised "an easy route for companies into the world of cyberspace" and its clients ranged from suppliers of British sports car parts to designers of table-top topiary.

Above: The Heaven's Gate logo, designed in typical early-Internet style. The cult earned much of their income from web design.

Opposite: Bodies being removed after the mass suicide at Rancho Sante Fe, San Diego, 1997.

Having decided upon suicide, the cult members prepared themselves for what they clearly believed would be a galactic journey timed to the arrival of Hale-Bopp. Each made a short video statement about how and why they were about to leave the Earth, after which they visited a pizza parlour and went to the cinema. When found, the victims were lying neatly on their bunks with their passports and IDs placed in the top pockets of their pyjamas, along with $5 dollar bills and small change. Carefully packed suitcases stood awaiting collection. The deaths took place over a period of days in three separate waves, the victims swallowing a lethal cocktail of vodka and Phenobarbital with a meal of pudding and apple sauce, then placing black plastic bags over their heads. The last survivors removed the bags and draped the corpses with purple triangular-shaped scarves before ending their own lives. They had kept meticulous records of their finances, paid their advanced accommodation rent and even a library fine of $2.50.

In September 1999, the suicide-pact house at Rancho

"*Man after man, his veins throbbing with the music, his eyes fascinated by the sight of the streaming blood, flung his garments from him, leaped forth with a shout, and seizing one of the swords which stood ready for the purpose, castrated himself on the spot. Then he ran through the city, holding the bloody pieces in his hand.*"

***The Golden Bough**, James Frazer*

Santa Fe was purchased for US$668,000 by a real estate developer and subsequently demolished. The memorabilia it had contained, including bunk beds on which the suicide victims had died, were sold off in a grotesquely morbid auction. Little remains of the group. One of the only survivors of the suicide pact, Rio DiAngelo, also known as Neody, the man who discovered the evidence, gave a news interview in 2002 during which he claimed that he was the sole remaining messenger of the cult.

Above left: Marshall Applewhite sat far right, with Bonnie Nettles next to him, around the time of his alien abduction prophecy.

THE RAËLIANS

The Raëlians represent another space-age religious movement that claims to "inform, not to convince, the public of its message" and whose members believe that the end of the world is not far distant. The cult was founded in 1973 by a French journalist and professional racing driver-cum-UFO writer, Claude Vorilhon, who now lives in Canada.

Having adopted the spiritual name "Raël", he claims his organization to be represented in 80 countries worldwide ,enjoying a membership of over 40,000. The Raëlians stand as a strongly UFO-orientated movement, which has taken the convictions of its founder about "techno-religion" to extreme lengths.

With its International Headquarters in Geneva, Switzerland, the Raëlian doctrine is based on the assertion that, on 13 December 1973, Vorilhon was contacted by an extraterrestrial intelligence and instructed to build an embassy at which "the ones who made all life on earth and whom humanity has mistaken for Gods" would shortly make official contact. Human beings, this emissary from some distant planet explained, have become

sufficiently sophisticated and technologically mature that we are now able to understand our creators rationally instead of treating them with mystery and dumb adoration. The extraterrestrials, to which the Hebrew word *Elohim* meaning "gods" has been conveniently tagged, concluded that Vorilhon, a French sports journalist, was the ideal ambassador with whom to make contact and to pass on their "final message" throughout the world.

Aside from journalistic and racing car experience, Vorilhon's particular qualifications are not clearly defined by the Raëlian press but it is suggested that on Christmas Day, 1945, just before the atom bomb was dropped on Hiroshima (the relevance of this incident is equally vague), the Elohim abducted his mother into a spaceship, inseminated her and erased any memory of the experience. The infant Claude was born of this celestial union on 30 December 1946. In 1973, when he received the divine message, he was persuaded to abandon journalism and concentrate on preparing the world for the arrival of the extraterrestrials. This was to be achieved through delivering "Sensual Mediation" seminars around the world so we might "develop our potential, our individuality and our common humanity" in good time before the Elohim turned up. In return, it is claimed they will give the benefit of their advanced wisdom and technology to earthly political and scientific leaders. The venue for these exchanges will be a special embassy which, according to some reports, is planned on the outskirts of Jerusalem but with the protection of internationally recognized neutral territory. The job of design and construction has been entrusted to Raël.

In order to fund the construction programme, Raëlian members are invited to make financial contributions. The level of donation is claimed to be at their own discretion but a guideline of 3 per cent of net income is recommended, with a minimum payment of $50 per annum. If members wish to take advantage of what is described, somewhat obscurely, as the "additional benefit of membership in the Raëlian Religion", they are recommended to contribute a further 7 per cent of net income.

Once accepted as members, Raëlians may work through six levels of responsibility "according to their own level of talent and commitment". These grades range from organizers, assistants, through full organizers, guides, senior guides and a single higher administrator at the apex of the triangle who may hold the post for seven years. Would-be guides can join the Raëlians immediately through the cult's website and attend the next available seminar.

According to Raëlian philosophy, which includes quasi-scientific religious jargon mixed with elements of hedonism, everything in existence is cyclical and every action a response to stimuli. Elohim are pockets of the universe with self-awareness. The Raëlian symbol represents, at its apex, galaxies within galaxies within the particles of our atoms and the opposite side the huge atom of which our galaxy is a minute particle. Within this framework we are simply atoms, all in a pure energetically organized movement.

By reading the handbook or attending a seminar, where the opportunity exists to meet people from all over the world in love and harmony, Sensual Meditation can awaken the mind and body and help to rid oneself of inconsistent values, which obstruct permanent harmony with the infinite. The process can be achieved by questioning of personal values and the actions which stem from them. It allows us to be uninhibited and to enjoy every sensation with a maximum of love and pleasure and without the paralysis of guilt.

In March 1999, following the conference in Vienna of the Organization for the Security and Co-operation in Europe, the Raëlians launched a well-publicized attack on the "anti-sectarian policies" of France, Germany, Austria and Belgium, which they accused of waging political war against minority religions labelled as "dangerous and harmful sects". In May of the same year, the organization also came out strongly against the "illegal NATO bombings of the former Yugoslavia".

The sect supports organ donation and has proclaimed the benefits of genetically modified foods. Claude Raël, as he now prefers to be known, founded Clonaid, which in the late 1990s claimed to be the world's first human cloning company and whose scientific director is named as Brigitte Boisselier. Through Clonaid, the Raëlian movement is sponsoring an American researcher who declares that "cloning is the way which will allow Man to gain eternal life thereby becoming equal to God as the Scriptures announced".

Around that time, Raël also wrote a book entitled *The Final Message*, a work that received lavish praise from within the Raëlian movement. A comment attributed to the film actor, Michael York, asserted, "If this book is a work of imagination, it ranks alongside the most inspired and breathtaking of fiction. If, however, its contents are true, its import is of extraordinary, earth-shaking significance."

Today, the "International Raëlian Movement" runs a website on which Claude Vorihlon's message appears to remain the central plank of the cult. Now described as a "Message from the Designers", the homepage of the organization provides a glowing assurance that "The Raëlian Revolution is boldly bringing about a complete paradigm shift on our planet. The Messages given to Raël by our human Creators from space contain the world's most fearlessly individualistic philosophy of love, peace, and non-conformism: a beautiful combination of spirituality, sensuality, and science."

Opposite: Rael cult Free Love Camp, France, 1992.

THE APOTHEOSIS OF ELVIS

Many cults verge on the bizarre in their rationale (or lack of it), but none can be more so than that surrounding the late Elvis Presley, whose memory has undergone an improbable degree of apotheosis since his death on 16 August 1977.

How is it that a 42-year-old, faded rock 'n' roll singer, his body bloated and wrecked by prescription drugs, who died from heart failure on his bathroom floor, has become akin to a transcendent god in the minds of his fans?

There have been arguments about whether Elvism, as the phenomenon is popularly known, amounts to a religion or a cult. Irrespective of the finer points of semantics, however, Elvism has many of the trappings of religion in that it worships a figure acknowledged by followers to possess some form of divinity. Sceptics on this score could do worse than go to a website described as "The First Presleyterian Church of Elvis the Divine". Here, they will be greeted by an icon depicting a haloed and pre-obese Elvis Presley suspended from a hybrid guitar-crucifix, wearing a loincloth held up by a rhinestone-encrusted belt. They will also be offered the encouraging advice, "Click on the King to enter the Church". To what extent these sites are serious is open to debate. Another website, that of the "First Church of Jesus Christ, Elvis", certainly contains more than a hint of parody. The homepage opens to reveal a portrait of Elvis in a blue robe, hand raised in benefaction, his heart radiating beams of spiritual light, with a pseudo-Biblical quotation: "For unto you is born this day, in the city of Memphis, a Presley which is Elvis the King". It also parodies a misquote of the opening of the John Gospel: "In the beginning there was the Word and the Word was Elvis". This site does, however, come clean about its tongue-in-cheek position when it declares that "He very pointedly did not rise from the dead three days later, but was nevertheless seen across the world by various and sundry housewives."

Parody or not, and aside from the small factual error that Elvis only *died* in Memphis, Tennessee, and was born elsewhere, there is something almost sinister at work in these electronic shrines. Elvism may not be a religion in the proper sense of the word, but a cult it

certainly is and its members are joined by a common belief that Elvis Presley extends some form of spiritual power and benefaction from beyond the grave. Its members describe themselves as The Presleyite Disciples, or Elvites, and according to one of the ministers, Presley appeared to 12 of the founders in a vision from beyond the grave. "On the first anniversary of the King's passing we gathered together at Graceland. We were the first and the last tour group ever to be allowed upstairs. A woman named Jessica exclaimed, 'Elvis! If only you were here with us…' Before she could finish, a strong wind blew into the room, a haze formed that brightened to a blinding light, then the King appeared, exclaiming 'Thank you, thank you. Don't cry all the time, like you ain't nothing but a hound dog. I am here.'"

According to a First Presleyterian Church poll conducted recently, as many as 30 per cent of those questioned believe that Presley was a messenger from God, 23 per cent consider that he was better than Jesus and only 9 per cent regard the question as offensive or blasphemous. The First Presleyterian Church founders claim to have spent five years in developing doctrine and sacred rituals before going public. They claim that it is indeed a religion on the grounds that, "a cult is just what closed-minded people call a religion they don't like", and the doctrine centres on an Elvite Holy Trinity including "Dixie, the Battle Hymn of the Republic and Hush Little Baby". Ministerial advice includes a message for all those who are "lonesome tonight" and whose life is "all shook up" that they are able to check out of "Heartbreak Hotel" if only they accept Elvis as Lord and Saviour and adopt catchphrases like "No Elvis, no peace. Know Elvis, know peace."

Certainly not all of the circle of friends and acquaintances that Presley gained during his lifetime support these notions of apotheosis. One commentator, James Parsons, has suggested that Presley himself

would have abhorred the adulation and that he actually objected to being called "The King". He was, according to Parsons, a simple musician and a religious man who would find the idolatry of the Presleyite Disciples and others highly offensive and troubling.

There can be no doubt that Elvis Presley, the living singer, touched the lives and perhaps even the souls of many people. He was responsible for initiating a radical "rock 'n' roll" culture among the teenage young, and his style and presence paved the way for the sexual revolution that unfolded in the 1960s. According to the American author and journalist John Strausbaugh, one of whose books is titled *Reflections on the Birth of the Elvis*

Faith, "The day Elvis died people were already insisting that they would never let his memory die. Instinctively, they knew in that instant that they had to preserve his memory and pass it on to future generations." There is a more cynical school of thought that the Elvite cult, along with the myriad of grotesque Elvis impersonations that have sprung up *post-mortem*, is nothing more than an orchestrated and, at times, ghoulish device to keep money rolling into the Presley estate.

AHL US-SUNNAH WAL-JAMAA'AH

The name al-Qaeda has achieved international notoriety through the militant pronouncements of its Saudi Arabian inspiration, Osama bin Laden.

There is, however, no hard evidence to suggest that any of this is correct. More accurately, al-Qaeda represents a way of thinking, a mindset that is opposed to Western democratic values and that appeals ideologically to Muslim fundamentalists, who envisage the world's future in terms of a global state, or *khalifah*, functioning under and dictated by Islamic sharia law.

The names of the fundamentalist organizations that subscribe to al-Qaeda and strive to carry out its objectives are much less well known, but it is the proliferation of these that anti-terrorist and intellegence organizations around the world are more concerned with. Ahl us-Sunnah wal-Jamaa'ah is a name that may be unfamiliar to many readers, not least because it is comparatively new. But as terrorist and alleged terrorist organizations become outlawed, their tactics are to disperse and then regroup under new leadership and new titles.

To trace the origins of Ahl us-Sunnah wal-Jamaa'ah, which means "the Messenger and his Companions", one has to go back to the summer of 2003. At that time, a radical Islamic sect known as al-Muhajiroun was operating in and around London, led by the cleric and self-styled *sheikh*, Omar Bakri Muhammad, and the British Islamic activist Anjem Choudary. It came to prominence in the media after Omar Bakri went public in praise of the 9/11 hijackers. As early as the summer of 1998, Bakri had also gone public on what he claimed to be Osama bin Laden's objectives for a holy war against the USA and several of those who trained to fly the doomed aircraft were later linked with al-Muhajiroun. The consequence of these various activities, which were clearly not in the interests of British security, was that on 30 July 2003, anti-terrorist police officers raided the homes of Bakri in Edmonton, north-east London, and Choudary in Tottenham, north London. Subsequently, al-Muhajiroun issued a statement that the British government was

"sitting on a box of dynamite and have only themselves to blame if, after attacking the Islamic movements and Islamic scholars, it all blows up in their faces".

No arrests were made, but Prime Minister Tony Blair announced plans officially to ban al-Muhijaroun, said to have had some 35 active cells operating in various British towns. In October 2004, the sect was ostensibly disbanded by Omar Bakri Muhammad himself, who believed that the "writing was on the wall". He was correct in his thinking. On 12 August 2005, under the orders of Home Secretary Charles Clarke, Bakri found himself banned from returning to Britain after a trip to see his mother in Beirut after being a resident for more than 20 years.

Bakri had correctly anticipated the turn of events and appears to have had contingency plans well laid. Some time after he dissolved al-Muhijaroun a new, shadowy organization made its presence felt in the UK, going under the title of al-Firqat un-Naajiyah, otherwise referred to variously as The Saved Sect or The Saviour Sect.

Its name apparently arises from a *hadith* or tradition ascribed to the Prophet Muhammad: "My nation will be divided into 73 sects; all of them will be in the Fire except for one" (by implication the sect that is saved). To add to the uncertainty about what had happened to former al-Muhajiroun supporters in the UK, another sect emerged at roughly the same time as al-Firqat un-Naajiyah. Whether this group, going under the title of al-Ghurabaa, "The Strangers", was a distinct organization, or al-Firqat un-Naajiyah by another name, is unclear. It appears, however, that the two became combined or at least re-established in November 2005 under the new name Ahl us-Sunnah wal-Jamaa'ah. The newly-named sect was launched in a north London charity shop amid claims that its teachings were those of as-Salaf us-Saalij, the "Pious Forebears", or companions of the Prophet. The launch was attended by Anjem

Choudary, a close colleague of Omar Bakri Muhammad in the senior leadership ranks of the old al-Muhajiroun organization, and other notable radicals including Abu Yahya, Abu Izzadeen and Abu Izair, although Omar Bakri Muhammad was excluded and declared not to be on "the consultative committee". At the inauguration, however, Simon Sulayman Keeler, a British Islamic convert among Ahl us-Sunnah wal-Jamaa'ah's other leading lights, described Queen Elizabeth II as "an enemy of Islam", since she was the head of a country that attacked Muslims. Keeler, from Crawley in Sussex, told BBC reporter Richard Wilson in an interview that he believes overturning a democratic government and imposing sharia law would be a force for good in Britain and rejects what he calls the "secular" approach adopted by the vast majority of British Muslims.

Under the name Al-Ghurabaa, the organization has issued statements protesting that its members "do not glorify any acts of terrorism, whether committed by individuals, organizations or nation states such as the USA or UK; we do not wish anybody to emulate them or praise them and make it expressly clear that it is not the intention of any of our articles or comments of our representatives. If anyone was to mistakenly get this impression then that is not our intention and we will do everything we can to clarify the misunderstanding."

Not all of its members, however, appear to have been in sympathy with this position. After a cartoon of the Prophet Muhammad was published in Denmark, al-Ghurabaa orchestrated a protest march from the Central London Mosque to the Danish Embassy, where placards were hoisted threatening suicide bombings and massacres with such blatant exhortations to kill as "Europe you will pay, your 9/11 is on the way" and "Butcher those who mock Islam".

When questioned about the placards, Anjem Choudary insisted that he did not know who had written the words. However, the al-Ghurabaa website also published a similar warning entitled "Kill those who insult the Prophet Muhammad". The subsquent paragraphs declared that "The insulting of the Messenger Muhammad is something that the Muslims cannot and will not tolerate and the punishment in Islam for the one who does so is death. This is the sunnah of the Prophet and the verdict of Islam upon such people, one that any Muslim is able [to] execute".

The new organization Ahl us-Sunnah wal-Jamaa'ah has operated discreetly, communicating through an invitation-only Internet site, and although its precise leadership is unknown, one of the more prominent contributors, going under the pseudonymn of Abou Luqman, has been Anjem Choudary.

Choudary is a 39-year-old solicitor from Ilford in Essex and the chairman of the Society of Muslim Lawyers. He is known to have founded several extremist organizations, some of which have now been banned, and has called for Britain to become an Islamic state, urging Muslims not to cooperate with the police in fighting terrorism. Choudary shows little reluctance about making inflammatory remarks to the British press. In 2004, he claimed that the Koran justifies the kidnapping and killing of Westerners in occupied Muslim lands and accused the murdered aid worker Margaret Hassan and UN election worker Annetta Flanigan of shoring up the occupation of Afghanistan and Iraq. The women, he said, "have only have themselves to blame. These people are all legitimate targets."

In 2006, wheels were finally set in motion to proscribe Ahl us-Sunnah wal-Jamaa'ah and the ban was ratified under fresh parliamentary legislation on 17 July 2006, when an order was laid down by the Home Secretary, John Reid, making it a criminal offence "to belong to or encourage support for the group, to arrange meetings in its support, or to wear clothes or carry articles in public indicating support or membership". It may well be, however, that Ahl us-Sunnah wal-Jamaa'ah remains one

step ahead of Reid and will simply change its clothes yet again. However, this did not stop Choudary, in September 2006, from reportedly making an indirect call for the assassination of the head of the Roman Catholic Church. Pope Benedict had made a speech the previous week, about which he later apologized, in which he quoted a medieval emperor who said the teachings of the Prophet Mohammad were "evil". Anjem Choudary allegedly told a crowd of around a hundred protestors that "Whoever insults the message of Muhammad is going to be subject to capital punishment … I am here to have a peaceful demonstration … but there may be people in Italy or other parts of the world who would carry that out. I think that warning needs to be understood by all people who want to insult Islam and want to insult the prophet of Islam." In October 2006, Choudary effectively repeated the message after addressing a university debate in Dublin. He compared the Pontiff's comments to those of controversial Dutch filmmaker, Theo van Gogh, who was murdered by a Muslim extremist in 2004. Choudary has also implied that Britain is heading toward civil war with its 1.6 million-strong Muslim community, saying, "We are reaching a situation where the Muslim community is increasingly under siege … I'm afraid of a Bosnia or Kosovo-style reality here in Great Britain."

Recently, a reporter from another press organization succeeded in infiltrating the Ahl us-Sunnah wal-Jamaa'ah website to discover that little has changed in the objectives. The site includes more calls for a holy war and militant recordings made by Osama bin Laden, Ayman al-Zawahiri and Omar Bakri Muhammad. In one video recording made by Bakri, he engages in advanced discussion about the bombings that subsequently took place on 7/7 in London. Omar Bakri is now reported to be actively participating in the forum on this website.

Opposite: Omar Bakri attending a sit-in demanding the disarming of the Shiite militant group Hezbollah.

TABLIGHI JAMAAT

Among Islamic fundamentalist movements, Tablighi Jamaat is hardly a new name. The sect was founded in 1927 at Mewat, not far from Delhi in India, by the cleric aulana Muhammad Ilyas Sahab Kandahlawi, who died in 1944.

It is based on a rigid brand of Islamic philosophy known as Deobandism, which was allegedly promoted as a reaction against British colonialism and is described as a revivalist movement, the name of which originates from a Muslim school or *madrassah* called Darul Uloom Deoband, in the town of that name in India. Ilyas' favourite slogan for the sect was "O Muslims! Be Muslims!" The chief purpose seems to have been to discourage former Hindu converts to Islam from practising a hybrid form of religion that still retained a considerable amount of Hindu culture and was supported by the British colonial authorities.

From the very outset, members of Tablighi Jamaat members were expected to pursue an extreme and radical interpretation of Sunni Islam and maintain strict adherence to *sharia* law.

The sect gained its strongest following in Pakistan and achieved a major boost there when General Zia ul-Haq, who ruled the country as a military dictator until 1988, encouraged its members to set out on a path of promoting fundamentalist Islamic policies.

However, from the 1980s, it is said to have become infiltrated by groups responsible for sectarian violence, including an organization known as Lashkar-e-Toiba,

Above: Russia's Federal Security Service detain suspected members of Tablighi Jamaat.

the so-called "Army of the Pure", which is fundamentally opposed to democracy and nationalism. Formed in 1990 in Kunar Province, Afghanistan, it was legally banned in Pakistan in 2002 and proscribed by the United Nations in 2005. The Taliban in Afghanistan are also said to follow the teachings of Deobandism, though critics claim that they subscribe to a very simplistic version.

In October 1995, high-ranking Tablighi officers in the Pakistani army formed a dissident group and were implicated in a plot to overthrow Prime Minister Benazir Bhutto, who was known for not being overly sympathetic to Islamic causes. Terrorist organizations such as Harkat ul-Mujahideen, formerly known as Harkat ul-Ansar and operating primarily in Kashmir, also make little secret of the fact that they recruit volunteers from the ranks of Tablighi Jamaat. Harkat ul-Mujahideen was founded at Raiwindi in 1980, its original membership almost exclusively made up of Tablighis, and since that time more than 6,000 Tablighi recruits have passed through its training camps. In 1995, it was linked to the slaying of several Western tourists in Kashmir. In December 1998, it hijacked an Air India passenger jet and forced the release of Masood Azhar, a major influence in the original Harkat ul-Ansar, who was jailed in India in 1994. Azhar went on to found the Jaish-e-Muhammad, a rival militant group promoting an even more radical line.

Tablighi Jamaat tends to shun media attention and publishes nothing about its activities, membership or finances. Overall, the organization has managed to maintain a high degree of secrecy about its operations, not least because it is run on a dynastic model – since 1944, a succession of leaders have been related to Ilyas, either as direct blood descendents or through marriage. What little is known of the internal structure includes information that an emir sits at the top of the hierarchy overseeing an advisory council or *shura*, which in turn delegates to local national groups that are expected to follow a strict code of Islamic law, including adherence to precise religious dogma, dress codes and practices.

The sect is influenced by a branch of Saudi Arabian Islam known as Wahhabism. Founded in the eighteenth century, Wahhabism, or Sulafism as its adherents prefer to call it, has pursued a near-fanatical course in matters of faith and religious practice. They see their role as the protectors of Islam against innovations that are considered heretical. Listening to music and watching television are outlawed, as are photographs or other depictions of human beings.

Although it does not solicit donations and claims to be self-funded, the Tablighi Jamaat organization is said to receive heavy financial support through various Wahhabi sources, most notably in Saudi Arabia. From the 1960s onward, the Tablighi adminstration used donations to establish active cells in much of Western Europe and north America and from the 1970s it broke into other areas of the globe, targetting impressionable young non-Muslims for conversion to Islam. It is reported that these Saudi-sourced funds currently facilitate the payment of high salaries to Tablighi Jamaat missionaries, operating most notably in sub-Saharan Africa, although the sect now operates in 150 countries and is thought to have an actively devout following of between 70 and 80 million people. Currently, it is estimated that as many as 15,000 Tablighi missionaries are active in the USA, where they are seen to pose an increasing security risk through their preaching of religious intolerance and extremism. One *imam* has described the organization as the Jehovah's Witnesses of Islam.

Each year, the organization holds mass conventions at Raiwind in Pakistan, Bhopal in India and near Dakar in Bangladesh that attract more than a million visitors each. It works hard to promote a peaceful image and its members insist that the organization has no involvement in terrorism, only in evangelism, encouraging Muslims to follow the example set by the Prophet Muhammad. However, there are strong and persistent claims that representatives of terrorist groups regularly approach students attending these conventions and invite them to undertake military training.

Although much of the focus has been in Pakistan, in recent decades the Tablighi Jamaat movement is reported by Western intelligence agencies to have also become a major force worldwide in the recruitment of young Muslim activists for terrorist operations.

By 2006, it represented a significant movement in Europe. Among the UK followers of the sect, the jailed shoe-bomber Richard Reid is known to have been a visitor to Tablighi meetings in England and two of the 7 July suicide bombers attended the mosque attached to Tablighi Jamaat's headquarters at Dewsbury in West Yorkshire. Tablighi Jamaat workers had at that time succeeded in attracting large numbers of young British Muslim men to rallies on a derelict industrial site near Stratford in east London, which included a temporary mosque. Followers who attend such events are exhorted to pursue what is described as "the effort". This allegedly involves signing up to travel around the country in groups known as *jama'ats* for between three and 10 days, with the intention of learning from each other and showing others at grass roots level the true path of Islam. This initial "effort" is followed up by a longer tour of duty around Europe for as long as 40 days and then a commitment up to four months. Each Jama'at includes anything from five to 20 members and one of the priority targets is now university campuses, where they are likely to have considerable influence among the impressionable young. The organization is reportedly a common link among several suspects arrested in England on 9 August 2006 over the alleged plot to blow up transatlantic airliners. Several of them are believed to have attended Tablighi religious study meetings and weekend camps.

Tablighi Jamaat is also notably active in France and a French authority on the sect, Marc Gaborieau, states that the final objective of the movement is "planned conquest of the world" in the spirit of jihad. In recent times, French intelligence officers have also described it as "the antechamber of fundamentalism".

While the sect continues to adopt an official line of condemning terrorism and claims to be non-political, a number of its members also concede that it is a global organization recruiting young Muslims from all walks of life and social groups, and that it is perhaps inevitable that some of these members gravitate toward terrorism.

In May 2005, a US intelligence analyst submitted a memo containing a summary of arguments for and against the continuing detention at Guatanamo Bay, Cuba, of Saad Masir Mukbi al Azani. A Yemeni by birth, al Azani had been arrested along with 14 others at an Arab guesthouse run by an "al Quaeda facilitator". The intelligence memo alleged that al Azani was a member of Tablighi Jamaat and that the organization was not only becoming increasingly radicalized but also had links to activities of terrorists, including those with allegiance to al Quaeda.

In summary, there appears to be some evidence that joining Tablighi Jamaat is the first step on the road to extremism for large numbers of young Muslim men.

Right: Aftermath of a bomb blast at Ahmedabad Railway Station in Gujarat, India, 2006.

KOPIMISM

The Missionary Church of Kopimism must rate as one of the most bizarre religious cults of modern times. Launched in Sweden, in January 2005, by a 19-year-old philosophy student – Isak Gerson – its title is derived from the word *kopia*, meaning to copy.

It describes itself as "a group of intellectuals fighting an ongoing war between copyright holders and the Imperialist Coalition Forces of the Internet". Kopimism emerged in the climate of a hotbed of online Swedish piracy and anti-copyright activism and its roots are to be found in an obscure Swedish political movement that translates, in English, as the Piracy Bureau, which later became known as the Pirate Bay.

In a January 2012 interview with *New Scientist*, Gerson explains that Kopimists meet on the Internet, where they share things with each other, their main objective being to keep all knowledge surviving and safe from destruction. The cult claims to subscribe to a New Age belief that is not concerned about a creator deity or any other conventional religious concepts such as afterlife, but regards information and the act of copying information to be sacred and therefore a form of worship.

In December 2012, Kopimism was accepted as a legitimate religion by the Swedish Legal, Financial and Administrative Services Agency after two previously failed attempts at recognition. From 2013 onward, online search queries about the cult are said to have risen dramatically. Some aficionados refute the idea that it is a religion and that information is in some manner divine. They claim instead that it is a necessary social evolution. Individuals can register online, and the cult is currently said to have more than 3,000 members worldwide. It is believed to have branches operating in at least 18 countries. Several Twitter accounts relating to the cult have been created, originating from countries as far apart as the United States, Canada, Turkey, Australia and New Zealand. These branches are permitted legitimately to interpret Kopimism in their own style as long as they meet the fundamental creed of the founder of sharing and enriching data.

The Kopimist logo takes the form of a letter "K" inside a pyramid, and the cult employs symbols, including other keyboard commands for copying and pasting. Anyone using the "K" symbol attached to their material on the Internet is allowing and encouraging such material to be copied. The basic tenets of the cult include, predictably, the termination of any copyright legislation and the legalization of all forms of data sharing. It does not promote illegal file sharing.

The cult organizers screen a video on YouTube, titled The Church of Kopimism, which lays claim to the religion being the first inspired by the Internet. However, the philosophy of the cult is drawn from a rather older source, the Biblical New Testament, and from a quote in 1 Corinthians 11:1, "Imitate me, just as I imitate Christ". This has been conveniently modified by Kopimists to read: "Copy me, my brothers, just as I copy Christ himself". There are no organized places of cult worship, and gatherings of members may either be physical or through the use of a server or the Internet. Such meetings involve religious practices of a kind in that they include worship of the value of information and copying it. Gerson argues: "Information is holy and copying is a sacrament. Information holds a value, in itself and in what it contains and the value multiplies through copying." He adds, "Because copying is the basis of the human thought process all of our ideas and inspirations come from conversations we have with other people and other people's art and culture."

The cult's website explains that to become a member of the missionary Church of Kopimism an individual must undergo a so-called rite by disclosing their personal data to the Church. They must then be seen to have copied the Kopimism symbol in order to complete the entrance test. There is no evidence that the cult is engaged in active

fundraising. However, when a request was posted that the cult publish its accounts online, the carefully worded response indicated that Kopimists do not believe there is an obligation to share all information all the time with everyone!

A Kopimist "Gospel" published in 2013 claims that in the beginning of the world the basic cellular elements, ribosomes, were created with the power to copy, in turn permitting the beginnings of life. For this reason, replication of information by humans is a form of godliness. Adherents subscribe to the idea of a force that keeps pulling the world in the right direction.

In 2012, the Missionary Church of Kopimism held its first wedding. This involved an Italian man and a Romanian woman, an official of the cult wearing a Guy Fawkes mask (a device used increasingly by cult devotees and anarchists alike to render anonymity) and a computer screen that read the vows.

SHERRY SHRINER

Sherry Shriner provides a trenchant example of how, through the media of radio and the Internet, one individual can command cultic allegiance, gathering large numbers of devoted and frequently young and impressionable followers.

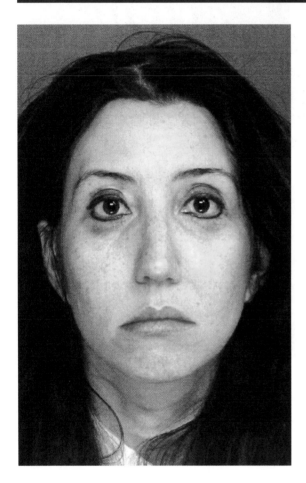

Shriner has been a popular albeit notorious radio show host, who broadcasted several times a week in America. In her programmes consistent themes included divine revelation, the presence of extraterrestrials and the end of the world. She described herself extravagantly as "Servant, Prophet, Ambassador, Daughter and Messenger of the Most High God". If that sounds a little pretentious, one of her various websites amplifies the qualification with the observation, "Just as my ancient grandfather King David stood against the Giants in his day with no fear, so will I stand against the Giants in these last days with no fear". Her beliefs were apocalyptic, with strong UFO overtones, yet she also strenuously denied being a cult leader. Shriner's reported death from heart failure in January 2018 in itself has stimulated all kinds of speculation about whether she has really died, was she simply an alien clone taken away by extraterrestrials, or was she, as she regularly claimed, on a US government hit list?

No independent corroboration of Sherry Shriner's death is readily available and, in reality, remarkably little in terms of hard fact seems to be known about her. She was born in Cleveland, Ohio, in 1965, according to some sources was married, and in addition to hosting her radio show was the author of several books with a common occult theme, including *Interview with the Devil, Bible Codes Revealed* and *Aliens on the Internet*.

Shriner's cult has had, and continues to exert, a considerable influence, particularly among the young, and her cult leadership has been achieved more or less exclusively through the medium of the ether. Her YouTube subscriber count was once said to be more than 6,000 and her videos have been watched in excess of a million times. The exploitation of YouTube for recruitment has been described as joining a cult without ever leaving the house, and is a trenchant example of how familiar tactics of exploitation and recruitment, especially of a younger generation, are increasingly being manipulated online.

Shriner's has by no means been the largest or the most recent online cult. It has not attracted followers in the magnitude of Raelism, the Moonies, or the Brethren, but among the lesser names, it has had, and still continues to exert, a considerable influence, particularly among the young. It also epitomizes the attraction of quasi-religious cults in the minds of the unwary.

Shriner has been described by critics as a paranoid mystic who used social media channels to recruit followers. She was, in essence, an online conspiracy theorist committed to the view that aliens, generally reptilian in appearance but posing as humans and known as the New World Order, are currently plotting to take over the Earth. This, with inventive variations, has been a fairly time-honoured thesis, but it is perhaps the first time that it has been promoted effectively through the Internet. Shriner pursued speculation, including Lucifer's infiltration of churches and government alike. One of her quoted claims was that: "The Earth is my battlefield … I don't belong here … I'm just working for the Most High God". This labour involved neutralizing aliens with a rock-like substance called Orgone, which can be purchased online through her websites in handy 3 oz, 5 oz, and 10 oz "blaster" sizes, along with special protective jewellery. Shriner's YouTube videos include such titles as *How to Kill a Zombie*. She asserts, confidently, that using Orgone Blasters will keep "chemtrails" from sticking over your home and area. The Orgone blasters will destroy aliens and demons, and other evil beings won't come near. Orgone, used in the recommended manner, also conveniently turns alien spaceships into fireballs that regularly crash to earth.

Shriner's cult has not been without its darker side. In 2017, it was linked to a notorious murder case involving cult members. One such cult member, Barbara Rogers, having claimed that she enjoyed eating raw steak, was accused by Shriner of being a reptile alien and duly excommunicated, along with her boyfriend, Steven Mineo. Rogers subsequently shot Mineo in the head, alleging to police that after Shriner had ostracized the couple Mineo had asked her to kill him. Shriner attributed responsibility for the death variously to the US government or to NATO.

A well-known cult education expert, Rick Ross, has put the dangers inherent in such organizations as Shriner's succinctly: "You're a parent and your kid is in his bedroom

and he's on his smartphone and he's in a cult and he's in your house. You're there watching Netflix and your kid is interfacing with cult members and a cult leader."

Above: The cover of Shriner's 2005 book, which claims to reveal "aliens in our midst" and expose alien networks.

Opposite: Devotee Barbara Roger's mugshot from Monroe County Correctional Facility, 2017.

THE TRUMPET CALL OF GOD

The background to this quasi-religious cult has proved hard to ascertain, but appears to be crafted very much in the mould of organizations including Heaven's Gate and Branch Davidian.

Its attraction is underpinned by a doomsday philosophy that the events presaged in the New Testament Book of Revelation are about to unfold. The majority of cult members have been instructed that they are part of a lucky chosen 144,000, who are to serve Christ during a so-called Tribulation period.

The Trumpet Call of God was founded by an American evangelist, Speed Rathbun, who later expanded his name to Speed T. Rathbun, and today prefers to be known by the Biblical name, Timothy. According to the United States Public Records Directory, his current address is in Hastings, Nebraska, where he lives with his wife, Amy. He alleges to be a prophet mediating between God and humankind through the regular receipt of divine instruction in "dream letters", the messages of which are then conveyed through such secular devices as YouTube. The content of these letters is generally posted on YouTube against a backdrop of comic-strip figures depicted in Biblical dress. The messages frequently contain very little of substance other than dire warnings of retribution for those who do not subscribe to the cult's strict religious code. They are generally composed in Biblical language. For example: "For behold, this dying generation ceases not from mocking My Word and those sent to them ... for all those who rebel against Me, and seek harm against My messengers, have made themselves meet for destruction!" Rathbun's audio messages are pitched in a similar hectoring mix of contemporary and formal King James Bible English.

Former members describe the cult as manipulative, requiring total obedience to the instruction of "elders", who discourage contact with the outside world. This is explained as "being separate" from those who are not of the cult persuasion, and who may therefore constitute "wicked unbelievers". It is reported that rigorous control is exercised over members receiving and answering phone calls and mail, and direct contact with family and friends is discouraged other than when a supervisor is present. Rathbun, it is alleged, claims that God requires complete separation from family members who are not cult members. Removal of cult members who do not comply is described figuratively as "exiting" or "expulsion from the Lord's banquet table".

The cult's ethic has been encapsulated as "trust with abandonment". Group study sessions in support of this reportedly take place three or four times a week, run through the medium of Skype. Each runs for about four hours, and is in addition to the requirement of "trumpeting" and personal study. Counselling sessions for new cult members establish if they can be classified as "feelers", "thinkers" or "doers". The psychological mind-bending is amplified through encouragement to dispense with worldly things such as secular reading matter, including newspapers and television, even to watching weather channels. Alleged miracles often occur after intense sessions of praying in order to encourage converts into following the correct path. Disclosure of past misdemeanours to other members is also encouraged. In short, nobody is permitted privacy. Rathbun is also said to issue prophecies on a fairly regular basis, few of which, if any, materialize. The distinct pitch of the overall message is that salvation is only possible through absolute compliance, and that leaving the cult guarantees spiritual downfall.

Rathbun's New Age salvation service appears to be at a cost, although he claims: "I have not accepted even one penny for the Letters and nor do I plan to... the Word of God is free to all!" Alleged requirements of the cult, however, include the payment of tithes. Rathbun encourages members to donate money through himself and his wife to certain undisclosed "international ministries" and advises that the Lord commands this of the flock. One ex-member of the cult states: "I gave money and even jewellery, because I didn't have enough money, out of fear

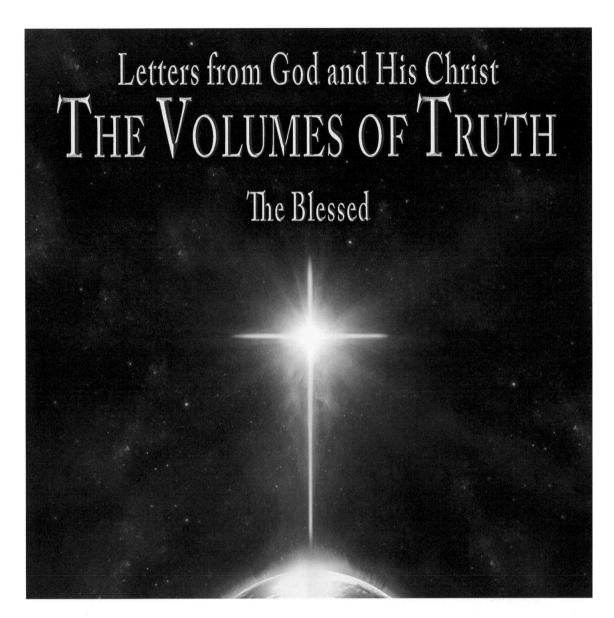

Letters from God and His Christ
THE VOLUMES OF TRUTH
The Blessed

that I would have to leave the group if I didn't give enough."

It has also proved difficult to establish exactly when and under what circumstances the cult was formed. It has been alleged that Rathbun and his wife earn $93,000 dollars a year through receipts from cult members, and that they own several properties in different parts of the United States. Another ex-member alleges that they paid Rathbun a monthly tithe amounting over a two-year period to more than $20,000. Other prophets within the cult include Trent Fuller and someone known as Jayse. The cult runs a Twitter account, has a profile on YouTube and a Dropbox account. The website Lulu also runs a page titled "The Volumes of Truth Official Bookstore". Rathbun's books, described as "Modern Scripture Spoken to this Generation", can be purchased at a special discount price of $14.24, for seven volumes in a handy compendium, delivered in three to five working days.

Above: The cult claim that Rathbun's books are "modern scripcture" for the modern generation.

TRIRATNA BUDDHAFIELD

The cult that operates under this title in the UK amounts to a meditative collective of Buddhists who run camping activities and promote retreats with interesting titles, including *The Alchemy of Friendship*, *Total Immersion* (for experienced meditators only) and *Sacred Landscape Yatra*.

Triratna Buddhafield originated in 1994 in a rented schoolhouse in London, under the leadership of Osho Leela. Today, it functions predominantly in the south of England. In 2000, its headquarters were transferred to Dorset, where it purchased a large country retreat, before expanding into Somerset, with the continuing purpose of both teaching and practising Buddhism and meditation. Currently, the cult also owns 17 acres of land on Dartmoor, further property at Broadhembury in Devon and at least one branch in Yorkshire. It describes itself as taking a leading role in developing an eco-Buddhist culture in England. Work on the land, mainly planting trees and clearing camping sites, is therefore an integral part of retreat activities.

The term "buddhafield" originates in the sutras of Mahayana Buddhism and refers to planes of perfect beauty created through the compassion of a Buddha. Buddhafield organizers in England work in association with the Triratna Buddhist Order. One of the best-known enterprises of the cult is the Buddhafield café, begun in the early 1990s as a fundraising venture to finance the cost of obtaining space at the Glastonbury Festival. Run by volunteers, the café, whose energy for lighting, cooking and heating is provided by solar power, functions as a not-for-profit festival enterprise, serving vegan and organically grown food. It is also said to provide a focal point for awareness at work and cultivates well-meaning impulses, as well as mindfulness in behaviour and talk.

In 2017, the Triratna Buddhafield charity, said to operate throughout England and Wales, enjoyed an income of £164,000. It is structured as a private limited company with a registered office listed as 2 New Farm Cottages, Itchen Down, Itchen Abbas, Winchester. The principal trustees are listed as Jeremy Bristol and Edward Tombs, and the cult leadership is said to consist of a group of Irish emigrants. At the helm is a 41-year-old former Dublin schoolteacher Wayne Bedford, who goes by the cult name Danaraja.

Operated under the guidance of the Western Buddhist Order, Buddhafield asserts that its activities function on a mandate system wherein each area of work is under the responsibility of a mandate holder, who in turn supervises a so-called consultative resource group. The cult's activities are open to people of all religious persuasions (festival participants may book on at £30 per day), and in addition to Buddhist teaching and workshops, festivals are said to include celebration of the connection with the land through live music, song and dance, yoga and meditation. The description of one of its events on the cult's website, a Green Earth Awakening Camp, typifies the flavour of much of its activity: "an off-grid, drug and alcohol-free, temporary community where creativity can weave and connections can deepen. Expect the opportunity to network and collaborate through discourse, movement, music, play and fireside story and song". Emphasis is also placed on ritual aspects of Mahayana Buddhism and at gatherings, there is always a strict veto on drugs and alcohol.

The UK registered charity Buddhafield should not be confused with a North American Buddhafield group of the same name that rose to prominence in the 1980s and achieved unwelcome notoriety more recently in 2016 after the release of a documentary called *Holy Hell*, made by Will Allen, a gay former member of the cult in California. The documentary was screened at the Sundance Film Festival, following which it went viral in both North America and Europe. Allen was employed as the cult's video producer, and in this role was able to document daily life inside the cult. He claims that he was regularly abused by the cult leader, Jaime Gomez, who allegedly has not infrequently abused other male members of the cult.

Gomez has assumed the name Michel Rosland and is chiefly known to his followers as Michel, but has also gone under several other names. He is a former ballet dancer who arrived in North America hoping to be a movie star, featured briefly in the cult classic *Rosemary's Baby*, but was then employed as an actor in gay porn films before becoming involved in healing and self-fulfilment. His precise spiritual beliefs remain unclear, but in video extracts he is frequently seen posing as a bronzed, muscular personality dressed in Speedo trunks and sunglasses. It has been reported that Gomez has now re-branded himself Reyjii or "God-king". The cult has also relocated to Hawaii and effectively "gone underground".

Opposite: A decorated tunnel leads to one of Buddhafield's annual community events, 2007.

WORLD PEACE AND UNIFICATION SANCTUARY CHURCH

It may seem far-fetched to read of members of a religious cult congregation turning up to worship toting high-powered automatic rifles as recommended accoutrements. This, however, is the instruction given to members of the so-called World Peace and Unification Sanctuary Church by its leader, Hyung Jin Moon.

If the name sounds familiar, it is because his father, Sun Myung Moon, was the founder of the Moonies, or to render its more ponderous title, the Holy Spirit Association for the Unification of World Christianity. The Moonies cult, in its heyday, functioned as a style of bizarre

dating agency with religious overtones. In 2008, however, Sun Myung Moon handed authority as "world president" to his son, Hyung Jin Moon. The organization had, by this time, become rebranded as the Family Federation for World Peace and Unification (FFWPU). Sun Myung

Moon died in 2012, shortly after which Hyung Jin Moon changed the title of the cult to the less cumbersome Unification Church. He also fell out with his mother, Hak Ja Han, known as "True Mother", who had given birth to 14 other siblings. She currently oversees the FFWPU and is said to enjoy a multi-million dollar lifestyle.

Hyung Jin Moon was removed from office and set up his own splinter movement in early 2013. This now operates from a former Catholic Church in Newfoundland, Pennsylvania, and has become known as the World Peace and Unification Sanctuary Church. According to its website, the cult members are awaiting "end times" and are doing so in the United States, Europe, Central America, North and Southern Africa, and South America.

In 2018, Hyung Jin Moon, also known for reasons that remain unclear as "Pastor Sean", gained a degree of notoriety when he supervised a ceremony in which the cult faithful of WPUSC were invited to renew their marriage vows. Promotional literature described this event as the "Cosmic True Parents of Heaven, Earth and Humanity Cheon Il Guk Book of Life Registration Blessing". A seemingly improbable feature of the blessing lay in Hyung Jin Moon's instruction to his congregation to come along wearing crowns fashioned from bullets and equipped with AR-15 rifles. This lightweight semi-automatic rifle is referred to blandly by the American Rifle Association as a modern sporting rifle and "the most popular rifle in America". As a mark of office, the leader personally carries a gold-plated AR-15. He likens these accoutrements to the "rod of iron" referred to in the Biblical Book of Revelation: "and he will rule them with a rod of iron".

In the language of the cult, all people are independent kings and queens in God's kingdom and "rod of iron" is no more than Bible-speak for the AR-15. Hyung Jin Moon readily advocates possession of guns as "religious weapons". The AR-15 has also been the lethal choice of armament in various mass shootings in the United States. At the time of Hyung Jin Moon's gun-toting marriage renewal celebrations, a nearby elementary school was forced to close for the day out of security fears. It was probably a prudent measure. The day following the cult's news release about bringing AR-15 rifles to the ceremony, the same choice of weapon was used in a mass high school shooting in Parkland, Florida. Hyung Jin Moon's sanguine response was to issue safety precautions, including the securing of rifle triggers with a zip tie. It has been reported independently that 77 per cent of white evangelic feel safer with a gun handy.

The homely website of the cult encourages recruits: "Experience the freedom that comes through a relationship with Christ. We believe that strong families, personal accountability and living for the sake of others are the building blocks of the Kingdom of God. At its last accounting period, the cult assets amounted to just short of half a million US dollars". The Moon family is reputed to have extensive business interests in the US, including ownership of hotels and gun stores. Tithes and offerings to the cult can be delivered via PayPal, major credit cards, cheques or bank drafts.

In the cult's expansive online literature, Hyung Jin Moon is described glowingly as, "a mysterious man who can fit himself to any given atmosphere and introduce Heavenly Father. He can let family members feel something new, and he and his wife are a beautiful couple who can show the flower of profound minds anywhere in the world". He is also reported to enjoy showing video clips to his congregation of more youthful cult members shooting rifles on the run in the woods, wearing camouflage for the Lord, and learning Filipino knife combat. This, he asserts, is about "practising to be deadly because you love people … the way of the rod of iron is the way of love".

Opposite: Hyung Jin 'Sean' Moon posing with his gold AR-15 at his home in Pennsylvania, 2018.

THE TEMPLE OF SATAN

The term "Satan" first appears in the Old Testament of the Bible to account for a demonic figure who seduces human beings into a state of sin.

The figure became common to all of the so-called Abrahamic religions and is typically drawn as a fallen angel, Lucifer, who rebelled against God and now commands a host of demons. However, in the twenty-first century, the term "Satanism" has lost much of its religious significance. Modern cults describing themselves as "satanic", most with not dissimilar remits, have arisen in various countries around the world, but the best-known today is probably the Temple of Satan, based in Salem, Massachusetts, famous for the witch trials of the seventeenth century!

Strictly non-theistic, the Temple of Satan does not subscribe to the existence of a supernatural entity, but operates more as a political activist group. Nevertheless, somewhat bizarrely, it employs satanic imagery in the promotion of its ideas of egalitarianism, social justice and the separation of Church and State. The cult was co-founded by Detroit-born Douglas Misicko, who changed his name to Lucien Greaves in response to numerous death threats. He is a Harvard graduate, who claims that the cult embraces rational inquiry removed from supernaturalism and archaic, tradition-based superstitions. One of its more controversial activities is a Protect Children Project under the claim that punishment meted out in school against students who are members of the cult is in violation of their civil rights. They earn the cult's support in seeking legal counsel in order to sue the offending school district. The cult's finances are unclear, but at least some of its revenue is earned through running an online Satanic Temple shop, where prospective members can purchase an official membership card for $25, a Satanic Temple Logo Mug in assorted colours for $25, or a hand-carved bronze logo pendant priced at $150.

The cult claims that Satan is a purely literary figure who stands for rationality, but it promotes itself not least through the imagery of the demonic goat, Baphomet. Based on notions of Lucifer, but not strictly of Biblical origin, Baphomet first came to prominence in the twelfth century to do with scandals concerning the Knights Templar. The deity resurfaced in the nineteenth century as a bizarre figure of occultism. Today, the cult possesses a bronze Baphomet statue in the shape of a muscular, part-human, part-winged "child-friendly" hermaphrodite goat, sheltering two smiling children. The one-ton figure was constructed at a cost of $100,000. Based on an image drawn in 1856 by the French occultist, Eliphas Levi, and known as the "Sabbatic Goat", it was first displayed in Detroit, in July 2015, by the local chapter of the cult. Seven hundred devotees attended the unveiling, each of whom was required to sell his soul to Satan before receiving a ticket. This was said to be a preventative measure to discourage more radical superstitious people who might try to undermine the event.

In recent times the cult has applied to have its Baphomet statue erected in the grounds of the Arkansas State Capitol, near a sculpture of the biblical Ten Commandments. This has been strongly opposed by Jason Rapert, a right-wing Arkansas politician, who asserts that "it will be a very cold day in Hell" before the installation is sanctioned. In August 2018, the cult delivered a riposte by mounting the nine-foot-high sculpture on a flatbed truck and parking it in front of the Arkansas State Capitol building for several hours. In November 2018, the Satanic Temple also attempted to sue Netflix for $50 million over its use of a likeness of the statue drama series *Chilling Adventures of Sabrina*. A settlement was reached for an undisclosed sum.

In the UK, an independently functioning cult, known as The Church of Rational Satanism, was founded by Les Banks in 2009. Googling "Les Banks" does not readily provide biographic information, but the cult is promoted,

Left: Lucien Greaves at the newly opened Satantic Temple international headquarters in Massachusetts, 2016.

expansively, as "one of the fastest accelerating satanic organisations". It claims to provide members with the philosophical foundations to take on board the archetype and shine as the unique individual you are in a conforming society, or as Banks describes it: "We are Rational Satanists; we know what it means to be truly enlightened in par with our true worldly views that can be backed up with reason, science, logic and cold hard fact." Advertised meeting places of the cult include the café bar area of the Royal Festival Hall and the Waiting Room in Deptford High Street, described as a "cool café". The cult website advises that it is simple to get involved, though involvement comes at a cost – the Deluxe affiliation pack will set you back £100. More modestly, you can obtain a membership card and either any single Church of Rational Satanism book, or a logoed T-shirt ("Diabolical Designs for the Left Hand Path") from the Rational Satanism store at £25 – all major credit cards accepted.

INDEX

CREDITS

The publishers would like to thank the following sources for their kind permission to reproduce the pictures in this book.

7 George Brich/AP/REX/Shutterstock, 10 Shutterstock, 13 Patrick Horvais/Gamma-Rapho via Getty Images, 14 Science History Images/Alamy Stock Photo, 17 Peter Horree/Alamy Stock Photo, 18 Frank Bach/Shutterstock, 21 Alfredo Dagli Orti/REX/Shutterstock, 22 Adam Eastland/Alamy Stock Photo, 25 Gianni Dagli Orti/REX/Shutterstock, 26 Valery Shanin/Shutterstock, 28 Werner Forman Archive/REX/Shutterstock, 31 Gianni Dagli Orti/REX/Shutterstock, 33 Granger/REX/Shutterstock, 34 Public Domain, 39 Granger/REX/Shutterstock, 40 Sergi Reboredo/Alamy Stock Photo, 42 Universal History Archive/Getty Images, 44 Granger Historical Picture Archive/Alamy Stock Photo, 46-47 Everett Historical/Shutterstock, 48 The University of Manchester, 50 GL Archive/Alamy Stock Photo, 53 Ettore Ferrari/EPA/REX/Shutterstock, 54 Granger Historical Picture Archive/Alamy Stock Photo, 56-57 Keystone Pictures USA/Alamy Stock Photo, 59 Marc Zakian/Alamy Stock Photo, 60 Chronicle/Alamy Stock Photo, 63 Keystone Pictures USA/Alamy Stock Photo, 64-65 George Brich/AP/REX/Shutterstock, 66-67 AP/REX/Shutterstock, 68-69 Ken Hawkins/Alamy Stock Photo, 71 Archive PL/Alamy Stock Photo, 72-73 FBI, 75 Sipa/REX/Shutterstock, 76-77 Damien Meyer/AFP/Getty Images, 79 Bernard Charlon/Gamma-Rapho via Getty Images, 80-81 Rainer Binder/ullstein bild via Getty Images, 82 The Asahi Shimbun via Getty Images, 84 Rick Bowmer/AP/REX/Shutterstock, 86 David Rose/REX/Shutterstock, 89 Paul White/AP/REX/Shutterstock,, 90 Andrea Delbo/Shutterstock, 92-93 Sipa/Rex/Shutterstock, 94-95 Lee Jin-Man/AP/REX/Shutterstock, 96 Pressmaster/Shutterstock, 101 Library of Congress, Washington, 102 Gianni Dagli Orti/REX/Shutterstock, 105 Charles Walker Collection/Alamy Stock Photo, 106 Niday Picture Library/Alamy Stock Photo, 109 Granger Historical Picture Archive/Alamy Stock Photo, 110 Charles Walker Collection/Alamy Stock Photo, 113 Granger/REX/Shutterstock, 115 Bettmann/Getty Images, 117 Walter Fischer/ullstein bild via Getty Images, 119 Steve Back/Daily Mail/REX/Shutterstock, 123 Ralph Morse/The LIFE Picture Collection/Getty Images, 1124-125 George Brich/AP/REX/Shutterstock, 126-127 AP/REX/Shutterstock, 128 Ken Lauder/REX/Shutterstock, 130 H. Christoph/ullstein bild via Getty Images, 131 Gilbert Uzan/Gamma-Rapho via Getty Images, 133 NUTAN/Gamma-Rapho via Getty Images, 134-135 Sipa/REX/Shutterstock, 136 AP/REX/Shutterstock, 139 Walter Oleksy/Alamy Stock Photo, 141 Georges DeKeerle/Sygma via Getty Images, 142 Don Hogan Charles/New York Times Co./Getty Images, 145 Stephane Ruet/Sygma via Getty Images, 146 Chung Sung-Jun/Getty Images, 149 Federal Bureau of Investigation via Getty Images, 152 Jiji PressAFP/Getty Images, 155 Sipa/REX/Shutterstock, 157 Paul Buck/AFP/Getty Images, 158 Fotex/REX/Shutterstock, 140 Guzelian/REX/Shutterstock, 142-143 Sipa/REX/Shutterstock, 164-165 Granger/REX/Shutterstock, 166 L Skilling/REX/Shutterstock, 169 Colin McConnell/Toronto Star via Getty Images, 171 Gail Orenstein/NurPhoto via Getty Images, 173 Mahmoud Zayyat/AFP/GettyImages, 174 Tass via Getty Images, 176-177 Shailesh Raval/The India Today Group/Getty Images, 178 Public Domain, 180 Monroe County Correctional Facility, 181-183 Private Collection, 184 Will Newitt/Alamy Stock Photo, 186 Bryan Anselm/Redux For The Washington Post via Getty Images, 189 Elise Amendola/AP/REX/Shutterstock

Every effort has been made to acknowledge correctly and contact the source and/or copyright holder of each picture and Carlton Publishing Group apologises for any unintentional errors or omissions, which will be corrected in future editions of this book.